Also by Donald Revell

Collections of Poetry

Pennyweight Windows: New & Selected Poems,
Alice James Books, 2005
My Mojave, Alice James Books, 2003
Arcady, Wesleyan University Press, 2002
There Are Three, Wesleyan University Press, 1998
Beautiful Shirt, Wesleyan University Press, 1994
Erasures, Wesleyan University Press, 1992
New Dark Ages, Wesleyan University Press, 1990
The Gaza of Winter, University of Georgia Press, 1988
From the Abandoned Cities, Harper & Row, 1983

Prose

Who Made the Eyes but I: The Art of Poetry,
Graywolf Press (forthcoming 2007)

Translations

*The Self-Dismembered Man: Selected Later Poems of
Guillaume Apollinaire,* Wesleyan University Press, 2004
Alcools, poems of Guillaume Apollinaire, Wesleyan University Press, 1995

Invisible Green

OMNIDAWN
RICHMOND, CALIFORNIA
2005

Invisible Green

Selected Prose of Donald Revell

Cover Art: Under the Elms
Artist: Fairfield Porter
Date: 1971-72
Medium: Oil on Canvas
Size: 62 $^5/_{16}$ x 46 $^1/_4$ inches Accession number: 1981.15
Courtesy of the Pennsylvania Academy of the Fine Arts, Philadelphia.
Gift of Mrs. Fairfield Porter

Cover and interior design by Ken Keegan.

Offset printed in the United States of America
on archival, acid-free recycled paper.
by Thomson-Shore, Inc, Dexter, Michigan.

Catalog-in-Publication data appear at the end of the book.

OMNIDAWN®

Published by Omnidawn Publishing.
Richmond, California
www.omnidawn.com
(800) 792-4957

ISBN-13: 978-1-890650-22-3
ISBN-10: 1-890650-22-6

9 8 7 6 5 4 3 2 1

Acknowledgements

The author wishes to thank editors from the following periodicals
and presses which offered these essays their first publication:

American Poetry Review
Asheville Poetry Review
Conjunctions
Paul Dry Books
Many Mountains Moving
The National Poetry Foundation
New England Review
The Teachers & Writers Collaborative
Verse

In memory of Patricia Wilcox

Table of Contents

Invisible Green

Methinks my own soul must be a bright invisible green

—Henry David Thoreau

I

Writing continues reading, returning action to the labors and delights of the day. (Returned to eternity, writing is prophecy, but to paraphrase Eckhart, I will not speak of that for now.) To see poems as the culmination of reading or of any process is to turn them against themselves, to make obstacles out of energies, shadows from daylight. Poems do not conduct their sunshine life among the Shades. The aesthete begrudges Orpheus his Eurydice. Yeats knew. The aesthete takes a mess of shadows for his meat.

> And when I looked, behold, an hand was sent unto me; and lo, a roll of a book was therein;
> And he spread it before me; and it was written within and without: and there was written therein lamentations, and mourning, and woe.
> Moreover he said unto me, Son of Man, eat that thou findest; eat this roll, and go speak unto the house of Israel.
> So I opened my mouth, and he caused me to eat that roll.
> (*Ezekiel* 2:9-10 and 3:1-2)

> And I went unto the angel and said unto him, Give me the little book. And he said unto me,
> Take it and eat it up; and it shall make thy belly bitter, but shall be in thy mouth sweet as honey.
> And I took the little book out of the angel's hand, and ate it up...
> (*Revelation* 10:9-10)

Poetry is the fate of reading, a phase of transformation. Ezekiel eats what God has written, incorporates the sacred as himself, and speaks out. The Muse is fuel. The man's book, the Book of Ezekiel, is a fire. St. John of the Revelation offers no scholium excepting a brief savor of bitter and of sweet. He builds instead, in the sequence poems know, a conflagration. Arts of obstruction esteem perceptions as products to be shaped, to be explained, to be shown off somehow, anyhow, as finally finished. Poetry is never finished. It continues and is consumed by what continues still. Perceptive reading never rests, and restlessness compels the further poem. Among the very oldest sanctities are the human rites of compulsion. (When Charles Olson wrote "I compel Gloucester," he was, in oh so many beautiful ways, honoring origins.) Poets compel their reading to come alive: conjury, not canon; act, not re-enactment. This has, in all ages, embarrassed the Formalist.

> Still less could Plutarch realize that what in his mind was
> a degradation, superstition in our sense, had been to his
> predecessors a vital reality, the real gist of their only possible
> religion. He deprecates the attitude of the superstitious
> man who enters the presence of his gods as though he were
> approaching the hole of a snake, and forgets that the hole of a
> snake had been to his ancestors, and indeed was still to many of
> his contemporaries, literally and actually the sanctuary of a god.
> …man gets in advance of the gods he has made, and is ashamed
> of the rites he once performed with complete confidence in
> their rightness. Then he tries by a cheat to reconcile his new
> view and his old custom. Religion, which once inspired the
> best in him, lags behind, expressing the worst.
> (Jane Ellen Harrison, *Prolegomena to*
> *the Study of Greek Religion*, 6-7 and 72)

Poor Plutarch was anxious about influences. Could the gorgeous formularies of ritual (could the ode? the sonnet? the elegy?) have begun as shouts into a snake's hole? If so, then aren't they somehow shouting still? To poets, this is the Delight of Influence: Whitman's yawp, Joyce's shout in the street, and Ginsberg's howl. Rites continue. A poem doesn't lag behind its gods. No, not if they're alive it doesn't.

> Till we become therefore all act as God is, we can never rest,
> nor ever be satisfied.
> (Thomas Traherne, *Centuries of Meditations:*
> *The Second Century*, 48)

The satisfactions of poetry arise from conduct, not from production. So even the most practical problems are potentially ethical ones, and there is no leisure for theory except in an unimaginable afterwards. No one hopes to outlive his gods, and no poet, I trust, aspires to survive the art of poetry. We go ensemble all the way in a moving space shared with the god, the poem, the beloved. This is what Maurice Blanchot describes as an "Orphic space."

> He (Orpheus) has life and truth only after the poem and because of it, and Eurydice represents nothing other than this magic dependence which outside the song makes him a shade and renders him free, alive, and sovereign only in the Orphic space, according to Orphic measure.
> (Maurice Blanchot, *The Space of Literature*, 172-173)

Think of "after the poem" as a consequence of reading, a further poem made necessary and delightful "because of it," alive by means which mean to continue and never to return Eurydice to the hateful Shades. The Shades are real all right, but nothing to do with poetry. (Even in Elysium, Aeneas discovered a "wild longing for the light of earth.") The dead bury the dead. Theory propounds an aftertime which love – for holy writ, for the holy imperative of writing the poem now and now and now – dispassionately ignores in the proper conduct of its passion. What Blanchot means by "Orpheus' gaze" I propose as reading and as the loveliest consequence thereof: poetry.

> Writing begins with Orpheus' gaze. And this gaze is the movement of desire that shatters the song's destiny, that disrupts concern for it, and in this inspired and careless decision reaches the origin, consecrates the song.
> (Blanchot 176)

I see a poem in its comely measures moving. Joining it, I begin myself to move, changing (disrupting, if you will) reading to writing. But reading continues, changes *with* me. *With* Orpheus, Eurydice builds a better fire than Hell. Consequences become origins so. Emerson knew, writing in "The American Scholar" that "We hear, that we may speak. The Arabian proverb says, 'A fig tree, looking on a fig tree, becometh fruitful.'" (Emerson 89). Real perception never rests.

The restless changes of reading to writing transpire in unstable equilibrium, just like stars, and like stars, they are innumerable at

19

any moment. But numberlessness remains real. As I make a poem, my reading continues everywhere in my words and in the verbal imaginations they constellate among themselves and me. I am too busy and I am not scholar enough to count them. It's all right. Whitman knew and told me never to mind.

> You will hardly know who I am or what I mean,
> But I shall be good health to you nevertheless,
> And filter and fibre your blood.
> ("Song of Myself" 52)

But sometimes, energies of exchange sparkle on the uppermost surface of a page. They instruct exactly as they sound, and the lesson is always: Act. In his first book, *A Week on the Concord and Merrimack Rivers* (in the "Wednesday" chapter devoted to principles and duties of friendship), Thoreau introduces a passage from the Confucian philosopher Mencius, in direct quotation.

> Mencius says, "If one loses a fowl or a dog, he knows well how to seek them again; if one loses the sentiments of his heart, he does not know how to seek them again... The duties of practical philosophy consist only in seeking after those sentiments of the heart which we have lost; that is all."
> (Thoreau 215)

The insistence is practical; the purpose is heartfelt. Thought, mindful of its duty, recovers our humanity. "That is all." Wit, inventiveness, and decorum, these go unremarked, maybe even unrewarded. And when he comes to write his masterpiece *Walden*, (the first and as yet unsurpassed handbook of American poetry), Thoreau has taken Mencius at his word and taken his imperative forward into the sunlight of a next new world and day.

> I long ago lost a hound, a bay horse, and a turtledove, and am still on their trail.
> (Thoreau 336)

Scholars have often argued the symbolic meaning of Thoreau's lost animals. The meaning is his message: Find them! Follow them, out of the book, into our own day.

A like imperative and sparkling begins *The Cantos* of Ezra Pound. "Canto I" does indeed open *in medias res*, but the *res* is not Ezra's but Homer's, and Pound does nothing to hide it. The writing of *The Cantos* starts from reading, and very early.

> And then went down to the ship,
> Set keel to breakers, forth on the godly sea, and
> We set up mast and sail on that swart ship,
> Bore sheep aboard her, and our bodies also
> Heavy with weeping, so winds from sternward
> Bore us on outward with bellying canvas,
> Circe's this craft, the trim-coifed goddess.
> Then sat we amidships, wind jamming the tiller,
> Thus with stretched sail, we went over sea till day's end.
> Sun to his slumber, shadows o'er all the ocean,
> Came we then to the bounds of deepest water,
> To the Kimmerian lands, and peopled cities
> Covered with close-webbed mist, unpierced ever
> With glitter of sun-rays
> Nor with stars stretched, nor looking back from heaven
> Swartest night stretched over wretched men there.
> The ocean flowing backward, came we then to the place
> Aforesaid by Circe.
> (Ezra Pound, *Selected Cantos*, 3)

Pound's Englishing of passages from *The Odyssey* (Book XI) is neither overture nor *tour de force*. It is practical and it is dutiful. Like Odysseus, even as Odysseus (the "I" of "Canto I" is Pound and the wandering king of Ithaka all at once), he makes pious consultation with the spirits of words prior to his own. Needing to go forward, Odysseus went down among the dead to find his way. It was a matter of survival and then of sunlight. Meaning to begin, Ezra Pound avows the fact and even the literal facticity of what he himself has dearly read.

Lie quiet Divus. I mean, that is Andreas Divus,
In officina Wecheli, 1538, out of Homer.
And he sailed, by Sirens and thence outward and away
And unto Circe.
        Venerandam,
In the Cretan's phrase, with the golden crown, Aphrodite,
Cypri munimenta sortita est, mirthful, orichalchi, with golden
Girdles and breast bands, thou with dark eyelids
Bearing the golden bough of Argicida. So that: ·
        (Pound 5)

Homer, and a translation of Homer into Latin circa 1538, and then
a welter of Latin, Greek, and Englishes old and modern: why? "So
that:" As with Thoreau's animals, the message comes straightforwardly
from turbulent symbols: Go on. It is a matter of survival, of piety
indistinguishable from the good employment of energy, from sunlight.

As reading continues in all writing, real attention, the best
purpose of poetry, means active mindful moving on. We labor in good
company: Orpheus, a fig tree, a turtle dove. A mind for the work
makes all the difference. I remember a terrible distinction between the
heroes Hektor and Aeneas. As each confronted the hour of his greatest
trial, each paused a moment to kiss his son. Little Astyanax screamed
at the sight of his helmeted father, and so Hektor

> ...lifted from his head the helmet
> and laid it in all its shining upon the ground. Then taking
> up his dear son he tossed him about in his arms, and kissed
> him...
>   (Homer's *Iliad*, VI, 472-474)

The later epic offers a less refractory but equally tender moment. Of
pious Aeneas, Virgil writes

> ...dressed in mail, he hugs Ascanius
> and through his helmet gently kisses him:
> "From me, my son, learn valor and true labor;
> from others learn of fortune..."
>   (Virgil's *Aeneid*, XII, 584-587)

Hektor, if only briefly, removed his helmet. Later he was killed, bequeathing his son a ruined city and an early death. Aeneas, more mindful of his purpose and so, I believe, more loving, kept his helmet on. He triumphed that same day, and he bequeathed Ascanius life and a continuing city. Hektor kisses in the past tense, Aeneas in the present. The poetry is the difference. In his poem "Heroes," Robert Creeley lifts the Virgilian imperative into our time.

> In all those stories the hero
> is beyond himself into the next
> thing, be it those labors
> of Hercules, or Aeneas going into death.
>
> I thought the instant of the one humanness
> in Virgil's plan of it
> was that it was of course human enough to die,
> yet to come back, as he said, *hoc opus, hic labor est.*
>
> That was the Cumaean Sibyl speaking.
> This is Robert Creeley, and Virgil
> is dead now two thousand years, yet Hercules
> and the *Aeneid*, yet all that industrious wis-
>
> dom lives in the way the mountains
> and the desert are waiting
> for the heroes, and death also
> can still propose the old labors.
> (Robert Creeley, *The Collected Poems*, 192)

The proposal is splendid restlessness, an urge for the further poem, "the next / thing." "That *was* the Cumaean Sibyl..." "This *is* Robert Creeley..." Exactly pious, but never overshadowed, Creeley sees actual mountains really waiting. Work is there.

Works Cited

Maurice Blanchot. *The Space of Literature,* trans. Ann Smock, University of Nebraska Press 1982.

Robert Creeley. *The Collected Poems.* University of California Press 1982.

Ralph Waldo Emerson. *Selected Essays,* ed. Larzer Ziff. Penguin 1982.

Jane Ellen Harrison. *Prolegomena to the Study of Greek Religion.* Princeton University Press 1991.

Homer. *The Iliad,* trans. Richmond Lattimore. University of Chicago Press 1951.

Ezra Pound. *Selected Cantos.* New Directions 1970.

Henry David Thoreau. *Henry David Thoreau,* ed. Robert F. Sayre. Literary Classics of the United States 1985.

Thomas Traherne. *Selected Poems and Prose,* ed. Alan Bradford. Penguin 1991.

Virgil. *The Aeneid,* trans. Allen Mandelbaum. Bantam 1972.

II

We must not look for poetry in poems. Poetry has further to go and greater occasions. As energy, it outspeeds the mass and manners of art, passing though words along the way to life. It is itself alive, and bursts from poems in actual ecstasy. ("Energy is Eternal Delight" – William Blake.) I want to write of ecstasy, the continuous motion of poetry out of confinements, out of poems. Poetry asserts the consequence of delight, i.e. an outside and worldly life where purposes are real, where methods are issues of morality. Poetry must be good. Blake made no idle allusion: "The Authors are in Eternity" (letter to Thomas Butts, April 25, 1803). In motion always, eternity is indistinguishable from creation, and there the link between ecstasy and ethics shines with sunshine life. Looking for poetry, we are moved to action brightly by action.

Jane Ellen Harrison, in her passion for source-work, evinced the actions of human art as energies seeking entirety.

> We have seen that art promotes a part of life, the spiritual, image-making side. But this side, wonderful though it is, is never the whole of actual life. There is always the practical side. The artist is always also a man. Now the aesthete tries to make his whole attitude artistic – that is, contemplative. He is always looking and prying and savouring, *savourant*, as he would say, when he ought to be living. The result is that there is nothing to *savourer*. All art springs by way of ritual out of keen emotion towards life, and even the power to appreciate art needs this emotional reality in the spectator. The aesthete leads at best a parasitic, artistic life, dogged always by death and corruption.
> (*Ancient Art and Ritual*, 215)

Anything less than life is not alive. Anything short of action is corruption. Poetry "springs" via the poem "towards life." To remain confined by an object of contemplative reading degrades poetry to parasitism, and in that state its powers dissipate and die. Death or ecstasy: there are no other options. And so again, ecstasy shows itself to be a practical matter. "The artist is always also a man," and as

Harrison's beautifully emphatic prepositions – "by" & "towards" – aver, when practice is human, practice is conduct, i.e. ethical. Without aesthetic immunity, poetry is real behavior, timely and first-hand. When value is worldly, poetry goes to the world.

> The one thing in the world, of value, is the active soul.
> (Ralph Waldo Emerson, "The American Scholar," 88)

Poetry, the soul of poems, does not reside or rest in them. It goes. We follow. We read to go where poetry has gone and to preserve the possibility of a delightful contact. In "The Poet," Emerson describes the ways of an ecstatic pursuit.

> The universe is the externization of the soul. Wherever the life is, that bursts into appearance around it.
> (266)

The beginning bursts. Soul seeks an outside, where poetry has led. Reality runs the risk of appearing.

> Every word was once a poem. Every new relation is a new word.
> (269)

The outside is unprecedented, and poetry has no word for it. But *in the delightful moment*, it finds a new word which is nothing less than itself, suddenly atoned. This kind of thing can happen. There are records: poems.

> Language is fossil poetry.
> (271)

There are records, but no rest. A fossil proves that life has gone. Faith adds a preposition: gone *on*. Poetry must be good faith.

> But nature has a higher end…than security, namely *ascension*…
> (272)

The italics are Emerson's. Faith is meant for bursting forth. Cast your eyes down for fossils. For poetry, look up. "for christ's sake, look *out* where yr going" – Robert Creeley, "I Know a Man." (The italics are mine.)

> For all symbols are fluxional; all language is vehicular and transitive, and is good, as ferries and horses are, for conveyance, not as farms and houses are, for homestead.
> (279)

It is good to be going. I mean, it is Good to be going. Some poems show the way.

> Art is the path of the creator to his work.
> (282)

Poems are not the work. They resound. They reflect. But sound and light continue with the real work which is energies and a timely life. Charles Olson shaped the Emersonian imperative to our own technology.

> The automobile / / has been hauled away.
> ("As the Dead Prey Upon Us")

> For there is a limit / to what a car / will do
> ("Letter 22")

We must not mistake the transport for delightful transportation.
   Sad are the intentional mistakes, ones meaning to captivate ecstasy in something no more beautiful than amber. "'Beauty is difficult, Yeats' said Aubrey Beardsley" (Ezra Pound, "Canto LXXX"). Beauty is the efflorescence of work. Neither wage nor franchise, it remains a property of work, and not a museum piece. Our literature offers a perfect parable.

> Every one has heard the story which has gone the round of New England, of a strong and beautiful bug which came out of the dry leaf of an old table of appletree wood, which had

stood in a farmer's kitchen for sixty years, first in Connecticut, and afterwards in Massachusetts, -- from an egg deposited in the living tree many years earlier still, as appeared by counting the annual layers beyond it; which was heard gnawing out for several weeks, hatched perchance by the heat of an urn. Who does not feel his faith in a resurrection and immortality strengthened by hearing of this?

(Henry David Thoreau, *Walden*, 587)

Such wonderful news: ecstasy is a fact of life. Delight is "a strong and beautiful bug." Describing despair, William Carlos Williams wrote (in *Spring and All*) "In my life the furniture eats me." Poetry eats the furniture, and then it flies off. And we, poor fools sometimes, stay in the kitchen shaking tables, imagining to make another bug. The sepulcher is empty, but the aesthete keeps praying there. Life is with the living, and still the formalist decorates a tomb. "Beauty is difficult, Yeats." Creation wastes no time on recreation.

The emotion to be expressed is the emotion of to-day, or better still, to-morrow. The mimetic dance arose not only chiefly out of reflection on the past; but out of either immediate joy or imminent fear or insistent hope for the future…If there is to be any true living art, it must arise, not from the contemplation of Greek statues, not from the revival of folk-songs, not even from the re-enacting of Greek plays, but from a keen emotion felt towards things and people living to-day, in modern conditions, including, among other and deeper forms of life, the haste and hurry of the modern street, the whirr of motor cars and aeroplanes…

…We may not cast reluctant eyes backwards; the world goes forward to new forms of life, and the Churches of to-day must and should become the Museums of to-morrow.

(Harrison, 236-237)

See how Jane Ellen Harrison emphasizes the "to" in "to-day" and in "to-morrow." I get a message from her prepositions. It rhymes with the egg in the dry leaf of *Walden's* table.

Action disables only backwardness. Ecstasy dispossesses idols of ourselves. We have nothing to lose and nothing to regret in the better excellence of working beyond works. Turning from the poem, poetry descries a further Way, an orientation to the outside that in turn becomes an outside too. I find a parallel in the Protestant soul and how Luther's "lonely church of one" can, by turning the way of poetry, delight to find itself alone with God. Such delight is the original genius of Jonathan Edwards, America's one-man Reformation.

> This I know not how to express otherwise, than by a calm, sweet abstraction of soul from all the concerns of this world; and sometimes a kind of vision, or fixed ideas and imaginations, of being alone in the mountains, or some solitary wilderness far from all mankind, sweetly conversing with Christ, and wrapt and swallowed up in God. The sense I had of divine things, would often of a sudden kindle up, as it were, a sweet burning in my heart; an ardour of soul, that I know not how to express.
> (*Personal Narrative*, 284)

Away from all concerns, Edwards finds conversation. Away from mankind (an *objet d'art* if ever there was one), he finds his Son of Man. Here is a practical instance of good ecstasy. It has nothing much to do with expression (i.e. a poem) because the heat, the kindling spark (i.e. poetry) is *outside*, and what it kindles is not an object (something crafted, like a little diorama with a 20-watt bulb inside), but a living heart exposed in the wilderness. Delight is wild. Joy prefers exposure to expression.

The wild consequence of work is a potent intimacy. I'd call it "redemptive," but as it retains potentials for eternity, I must not limit it to one and only one event. Exposed and externalized, with no poem intervening, the poet is alone with poetry. Craft is irrelevant. Audience is nowhere to be seen. It is *there*, in the wilderness of this holy intimacy, where conduct matters most. It is *there*, and inexpressibly, where conduct flames over. No contemporary shows this quite so clearly, quite so thrillingly, as Jack Spicer.

from *Ten Poems for Downbeat*

    5

I can't stand to see them shimmering in the impossible music of
the Star Spangled Banner. No
One accepts this system better than poets. Their hurts healed
for a few dollars.
Hunt
The right of animals. I can't. The poetry
Of the absurd comes through San Francisco television.
Directly connected with moon-rockets.
If this is dictation, it is driving
Me wild

    6

The poem begins to mirror itself.
    The identity of the poet gets more obvious.
Why can't we sing like nightingales? Because we're not
nightingales and can
    never become them. The poet has an arid parch of his
reality and the others.
Things desert him. I thought of you as a butterfly tonight with
clipped wings.
    (*The Collected Books of Jack Spicer*, 265)

Driven wild from the outside, Jack and poetry escape. "The poem"
and "Identity" remain behind with neither song nor wings. Poems
or poetry? Some choices don't even need to be made. The tombs are
empty. As Spicer said most famously, in his "Imaginary Elegies," "Poet /
Be like God." Ecstasy enjoys no company more.

Works Cited

William Blake. *Blake's Poetry and Designs*, eds. Mary Lynn Johnson and John E. Brant. W. W. Norton & Co., 1979.

Robert Creeley. *The Collected Poems of Robert Creeley*. University of California Press, 1982.

Jonathan Edwards. *A Jonathan Edwards Reader*, eds. John E. Smith, Harry S. Stout, and Kenneth P. Minkems. Yale University Press, 1995.

Ralph Waldo Emerson. *Selected Essays*, ed. Larzer Ziff. Penguin, 1982.

Jane Ellen Harrison. *Ancient Art and Ritual*. Oxford University Press, 1948.

Charles Olson. *Selected Writings*, ed. Robert Creeley. New Directions, 1967.

Ezra Pound. *The Cantos*. New Directions, 1970.

Jack Spicer. *The Collected Books of Jack Spicer*, ed. Robin Blaser. Black Sparrow Press, 1975.

Henry David Thoreau. *Henry David Thoreau*, ed. Robert Sayre. Literary Classics of the United States, 1985.

William Carlos Williams. *Imaginations*. New Directions, 1970.

III

Having been wilded (be-wildernessed) from the poem, what further? What next? Ecstasy is a various way and, in its aftermath, prolific still. Poetry does not go away. It goes on. I join it. We stick together. Whitman loved adhesiveness so because it is a friendly profusion. In the aftermath of ecstasy, poetry is my friend in Elysium, favoring and assisting to the end. And because Elysium is an interval (I do not take this only from *Aeneid VI*, but also from nights like last night, January 8, 2001, when a full moon shining down on black ice made a brief but heavenly place between darkness and daylight, and I spent time there), its end may be the next ephemeral and beautiful production, even a poem sometimes, but different, thanks to the friend. When I am writing, there is myself, and there is my subject or purpose. My friend makes three.

> Now when Jesus was risen early the first day of the week, he appeared first to Mary Magdalene, out of whom he had cast seven devils.
> And she went and told them that she had been with him, as they mourned and wept.
> And they, when they had heard that he was alive, and had been seen of her, believed not.
> After that he appeared in another form unto two of them, as they walked, and went into the country.
> And they went and told it unto the residue: neither believed they them.
> (Mark 16:9-13)

It is always long past time to acknowledge the wonderful company of a friend, the third one on the way to poems.

> Who is the third who walks always beside you?
> When I count, there are only you and I together
> But when I look ahead up the white road
> There is always another one walking beside you

Gliding wrapt in a brown mantle, hooded
I do not know whether a man or a woman
--But who is that on the other side of you?
        (T.S. Eliot, "The Waste Land," 360-366)

The third is countless and unaccountable unless I join him and keep pace. Otherwise, I lag behind in the debris and anthologies, rewriting, counting always only two.

    It takes three to make a child.
        (E.E. Cummings, *A Miscellany Revisited*, 330)

    …literature begins only when a third person is born in us that strips us of the power to say "I"…
        (Gilles Deleuze, *Essays Critical and Clinical*, 3)

Uncontrollably newborn, my friend, this third one, engages in nothing but birth and birth again. Under such instruction, poems are the morning news. The words wake. Myself and my purposes are speechlessly remade where the poetry thrives, and we thrive too.

    Why cavil at costs? Poems are difficulties. This fact shines through every passage, say, of Coleridge, and to good effect. Genius of the fragment, sole author and proprietor of that first avant-garde periodical, *The Friend*, Coleridge suffered the divide between joyful Work and barren Works, and, suffering, he crossed over. In "Dejection: An Ode," he made his desperate distinction rive.

    I see them all so excellently fair,
    I see, not feel, how beautiful they are!
        (37-38)

What is the use of eyes that only see? What good is an image to me without the feeling that befriends and moves us both?

    Hence, viper thoughts, that coil around my mind,
        Reality's dark dream!
        (94-95)

"Dejection: An Ode" measures exactly the agony of an absence. It wants the friend. And she is real, no dream: one Sara. Her absence abjects reality, and the bruised heel of the poet can only bruise the viper's head of his poem. Until:

> But hush! there is a pause of deepest silence!
> (114)

In silence comes the Elysian pause.

> And all that noise, as of a rushing crowd,
> With groans, and tremulous shudderings – all is over –
> (115-116)

Coleridge does not *solve* the problem of dejection. He is drawn away from it, delighted to find that life – one Sara – is elsewhere, where it is morning.

> With light heart may she rise,
>   Gay fancy, cheerful eyes,
> Joy lift her spirit, joy attune her voice;
> To her may all things live, from pole to pole,
> Their eddying of her living soul!
>   O simple spirit, guided from above,
> Dear Lady! friend devoutest of my choice,
> Thus mayest thou ever, evermore rejoice.
>   (132-139)

"Dejection: An Ode" thrives by denying the two sides of its name. It hates dejection, and it is no ode. All praise belongs to a third name, the friend's. Coleridge's self and titular purpose fall off. A newborn finds a friend. (N.B. Finding blesses, as blessing finds.) Newborn goes.

Our finest contemporary poets are all, in their varieties, Coleridgean adepts of the blessed, of the third name. I think of Barbara Guest who finds a prayer and friend in "An Emphasis Falls on Reality." Here a single "I" envies realism its wild and apt morphologies.

Clouds fields change into furniture
furniture metamorphizes into fields
an emphasis falls on reality.

"It snowed toward morning," a barcarole
the words stretched severely

silhouettes they arrived in trenchant cut
the face of lilies....

I was envious of fair realism.

I desired sunrise to revise itself
as apparition, majestic in evocativeness,
two fountains traced nearby on a lawn....

you call treatments
of "being" and "nothingness"
illuminations apt
to appear from variable directions –
they are orderly as motors
floating on the waterway,

so silence is pictorial
when silence is real.
      (1-19)

The friend's name is Emphasis, whose touch transforms a solitary
utterance – "I was envious of fair realism" – into many. Emphasis
falling on any word changes the whole and each, and so every word
governs a line of its own while nevertheless remaining a part. Such
circumstance must be the paradise of vocables, thanks to the friend.
Guest is one, Realism another. The bondage of equilibrium is broken
by a third agency, friendly and prolific. Ordinarily, an "I" makes
pictures, and reality resists the pictorial. This is the bad stalemate
of too many poems. In "An Emphasis Falls on Reality," though, as in
"Dejection : An Ode," all is freed, and by a silence. Emphasis has no

word of its own and can bless all: "so silence is pictorial / when silence is real." What merely balanced once now moves.

> The necessary idealizing of your reality
> is part of the search, the journey
> where two figures embrace
>
> This house was drawn for them
> it looks like a real house
> perhaps they will move in today
> into ephemeral dusk and
> move out of that into night
> selective night with trees,
>
> The dark copies of all trees.
> (36-45)

What good are images without the feeling (here, the *emphasis*) that befriends and moves them along with the image-maker? Guest is past the question. Necessity and ideality journey together in her poem, joined by a searching emphasis which makes their journey numerous and real. Mimesis, a term of two, is displaced by a better friend, a third traveler, whose selection always includes all.

Inclusiveness remains itself only through a constant breaking open into change. Ecstasy is, apart form us, a *perpetuum mobile*. And so the friend plays many parts, always making a third among first causes. It is typical of James Schuyler's wonderful humility that in his poem "The Bluet" the friend owns pride of place in the very first line. Schuyler's subject and persona follow after.

> And is it stamina
> that unseasonably freaks
> forth a bluet, a
> Quaker lady, by
> the lake? So small,
> a drop of sky that
> splashed and held,
> four-petalled, creamy

in its throat. The woods
around were brown,
the air crisp as a
Carr's table water
biscuit and smelt of
cider.

      (1-14)

Schuyler stands as a glad, unnecessary witness to an event – the
bluet's unseasonable flowering – made possible and then actually
made by "stamina." This is no ordinary poem about a flower. This
is not a nosegay. As emphasis activates the words of Barbara Guest,
here stamina seizes Schuyler's attention and sets it moving. There is
a poet, and there is a flower, their conventionally static relationship
emblematized in the folksy epithet "Quaker lady." Very nice. But
stamina will not be restrained, and so the poem moves outward, really
seeing *this* bluet and finding more and more ways to taste and see the
occasion transpiring now. The poem is called "The Bluet." But the
poetry, the friend, the third and vital agency, is stamina.
    And then, constant to change, the poetry is something else.

But that bluet was
the focus of it all: last
spring, next spring, what
does it matter? Unexpected
as a tear when someone
reads a poem you wrote
for him. "It's this line
here." That bluet breaks
me up, tiny spring flower
late, late in dour October.

      (25-34)

Eternity's timeliness breaks forth as a flower, and then it is a human
friend, someone breaking into tears because of a poem, a poem made
possible, perhaps, by some flower unseasonably breaking into bloom
and breaking a poet up. (See above: Cummings and Deleuze.) What is
stamina now? Something breaking, here *and* there. Not gone, but gone

40

on, poetry moves past the tender debris of the poem, keeping pace with an expected time: late October.

In Robert Creeley's "Bresson's Movies," the unexpected is eventually the reader's role and portion too. At first, the poem offers a common trope: an artist, moved by another's art, makes art in homage. The poem seems a poem "about," keenly enacting the details of a movie moving it.

> A movie of Robert
> Bresson's showed a yacht,
> at evening on the Seine,
> all its lights on, watched
>
> by two young, seemingly
> poor people, on a bridge adjacent,
> the classic boy and girl
> of the story, any one
>
> one cares to tell. So
> years pass, of course, but
> I identified with the young,
> embittered Frenchman,
>
> knew his almost complacent
> anguish and the distance
> he felt from his girl.
> (1-15)

To Bresson, add Creeley (a Robert to a Robert, as shown by the witty enjambment of lines one and two). The poem puts the poet in the picture, and a binary lyric system prepares to close. But not yet, not quite.

> Yet another film
>
> of Bresson's has the

aging Lancelot with his
awkward armor standing
in a woods, of small trees,

dazed, bleeding, both he
and his horse are,
trying to get back to
the castle, itself of

no great size. It
moved me, that
life was after all
like that. You are

in love. You stand
in the woods, with
a horse, bleeding.
The story is true.
(16-32)

Circumscription yields to continuity. The stable lyric is deranged,
shown "awkward," shown "dazed," shown "bleeding." As in "The Bluet,"
something breaks, and there are three: Bresson, Creeley, and a third.
Being so moved ("It / moved me"), "I" gives way to "you." Why?
Because "The story is true." "Bresson's Movies" belongs to humane
experience, a canon of much much more than poems. Here, the
third and friendly agency is truth, and truth is, after all, with us, the
readers, the "you." In the time of the poem, intensified now at the end
by a beautiful influx of prepositions – "in," "in," "with" – truth must
be ourselves in evidence and *as* evidence. Lancelot alone is a legend.
The testimony of Creeley's closing words is borne OUT only by each
reader's knowing, in his own sovereign actual wounds, that it is true.
We are the poem's friend now, and so, for a while, we and poetry are
one.

And there are poems to celebrate this good union. John Ashbery,
in "A Blessing in Disguise," has written a fast, sure prothalamion for
the sometime wedding of oneself to the free friend, to poetry. It is like
an accelerated or imploded dejection ode. In it, an "I" confined to sad,

sole argument suddenly finds a way beyond argument: unexpected nuptials, wild and free.

> Yes, they are alive and can have those colors,
> But I, in my soul, am alive too.
> I feel I must sing and dance, to tell
> Of this in a way, that knowing you may be drawn to me.
>
> And I sing amid despair and isolation
> Of the chance to know you, to sing of me
> Which are you. You see,
> You hold me up to the light in a way
>
> I should never have expected, or suspected, perhaps
> Because you always tell me I am you,
> And right. The great spruces loom.
> I am yours to die with, to desire.
>   (1-12)

Quickly, poetry shatters an unmoving discourse between the self and its despairs. The unsuspected friend stares gigantically up at a poet freely taken into hand. Prismatic, not imprisoned there, Ashbery finds many more than one in every one. Deleuze was right, and the momentous births go far.

> I cannot ever think of me, I desire you
> For a room in which the chairs ever
> Have their backs turned to the light
> Inflicted on the stone and paths, the real trees
>
> That seem to shine at me through a lattice toward you.
> If the wild light of this January day is true
> I pledge me to be truthful unto you
> Whom I cannot ever stop remembering.

Remembering to forgive. Remember to pass beyond you into the day
On the wings of the secret you will never know.
Taking me from myself, in the path
Which the pastel girth of the day has assigned to me.

I prefer "you" in the plural, I want "you,"
You must come to me, all golden and pale
Like the dew and the air.
And then I start getting this feeling of exaltation.
        (13-28)

Ecstasy pluralizes. Here is a poem the poet escapes. "'You' in the plural" is poetry and we. One aftermath of ecstasy is more ecstasy, even wilder than before – "this feeling of exaltation." Where is the poem now? Dew and air. Sometimes poetry keeps us when it goes. Sometimes it keeps even everybody.

Works Cited

John Ashbery. *Rivers and Mountains.* New York: Holt, Rinehart and Winston, 1966.

Samuel Taylor Coleridge. *Selected Poems,* ed. Richard Holmes. London: Penguin Books Ltd., 1996.

Robert Creeley. *Mirrors.* New York: New Directions, 1983.

E.E. Cummings. *A Miscellany Revisited.* New York: October House, 1965.

Gilles Deleuze. *Essays Critical and Clinical,* trans. Daniel W. Smith and Michael A. Greco. Minneapolis: University of Minnesota Press, 1997.

T.S. Eliot. *Selected Poems.* New York: Harcourt, Brace & World, 1936.

Barbara Guest. *Selected Poems.* Los Angeles: Sun & Moon Press, 1995.

James Schuyler. *Collected Poems.* New York: Farrar, Straus & Giroux, 1993.

Henry David Thoreau. *Henry David Thoreau,* ed. Robert Sayre. New York: Literary Classics of the United States, 1985.

IV

We never tire of ecstasy: not in sleep, not even in death. At night, as Jeffers knew, even the whole republic shines, perishing into its ecstatic geography. And in the morning, evidenced by dandelions and violets thick on the playfields mown so closely yesterday, the news is of something very wild and free. The ground is silver-beaded, though there has been no rain. There has been progress and sweat overnight. Our sleep was obvious, like the darkness, like stillness on the roads, but nothing was still. Rites continued dearly. What's to know, and how?

> In some measure or other, progress is always a transcendence of what is obvious.
> (Alfred North Whitehead, *Process and Reality*, 14)

One night last week, I fell asleep beside my son. Our bedtime reading was a *Book of Spiders*, as it had been for some while. I was surprised that night to have a beautiful dream of Ezra Pound. (I wish I dreamed about him more. The event is always herald of some help and a good idea. And I love his face, solemnly mischievous, like a fiddle.) In my dream, the great poet shuffled through a field, stopping often to look into the high grass. Shadows of big clouds moved and made the field seem oceanic. Pound called out, a yip of delight, and called me over. He showed me something he had found. It was a spider, smiling. (Disney vs. the Metaphysicals?) Next morning, after my son was off to Longfellow Elementary, I sought a connection between the *Book of Spiders* and my dream. I remembered plenty of bugs from *The Pisan Cantos*, and sure enough, spider appears in the very first one, "Canto LXXIV."

> Arachne mi porta fortuna

Good luck is a good reason for smiling, I suppose. And spider returns, more busily and explicit, in "Canto LXXVI."

> Arachne, che mi porta fortuna, go spin on that tent rope

47

As Pound avers in "Canto LXXIV," "with one day's reading a man may have the key in his hands." I had a clue, but hardly a key. I mean, what good fortune (what smile) did spider bring to the old man confined to a gorilla cage, charged with treason because of his scurrilous broadcasts, awaiting disgraceful death? What delighted Ezra so in Pisa and in my dream? The only solution to reading is to read more. Such reasoning makes experimental writing. Again from Whitehead:

> Rationalism never shakes off its status of an experimental adventure.
> (Whitehead, 14)

The American precursor of any poet's joy in spiders is the 20 year old Jonathan Edwards who, on Halloween day, 1723, wrote what has come to be know as "The Spider Letter." There, the inchoate theologian details a reasonable experiment of his delighted eyes.

> …But, sir, I have often seen that which is yet more astonishing. In a very calm serene day in the forementioned time of year, standing at some distance between the end of an house or some other opaque body, so as just to hide the disk of the sun and keep off his dazzling rays, and looking along close by the side of it, I have seen vast multitudes of little shining webs and glistening strings, brightly reflecting the sunbeams, and some of them of a great length, and at such a height that one would think that they were tacked to the vault of the heavens, and would be burnt like tow in the sun, making a very pleasing as well as surprising appearance. It is wonderful at what a distance these webs may plainly be seen in such a position to the sunbeams, which are so fine that they cannot be seen in another position, though held near to the eye; some that are at a great distance appear (it cannot be otherwise) several thousands of times as big as they ought: They doubtless appear under as great an angle as a body of a foot diameter ought to do at such a distance; so greatly doth coruscation increase the apparent bigness of bodies at a distance, as is observed in the fixed stars. But that which is most astonishing is that very often there appears at the end of these webs, spiders sailing

in the air with them, doubtless with abundance of pleasure, though not with so much as I have beheld them and shown them to others. And since I have seen these things I have been very conversant with spiders.

(Jonathan Edwards, *A Jonathan Edwards Reader*, 1-2)

Here is a tone in harmonic anticipation of Pound's in Pisa: astonished serenity. The superabundant pleasure of sight becomes conversation. And in the adventure of conversation, wisdom begins to show, and peace. Seeing that the spiders take visible pleasure from their acrobatics (as in, perhaps, "Arachne, che mi porta fortuna, go spin on that tent rope"), Edwards gains a good and comfortable insight into the nature of his God.

...Hence the exuberant goodness of the Creator, who hath not only provided for all the necessities, but also for the pleasure and recreation of all sorts of creatures, even the insects.

(Edwards, 5)

All necessities and more are freely offered by facts of life. Yet Edwards, even so early, chooses to pursue the experiment of sight farther than first fact, all the way to its continuous origin. Poetry is past comfort. It is busy with the world. And so Edwards sends his eyesight forth with the spiders, seeing them swing themselves the whole way to the ocean. They drown there, making way for the refreshment and increase of their kind.

...The reason of their flying at that time of year I take to be because the ground and trees and grass, the places of their residence in summer, begin to be chill and uncomfortable. Therefore when the sun shines pretty warm they leave them, and mount up into the air and expand their wings to the sun, and flying for nothing but their own ease and comfort, they suffer themselves to go that way that they can go with the greatest ease, and so where the wind pleases: and it being warmth they fly for, they never fly against the wind nor sidewise to it, they find it cold and laborious; they therefore seem to use their wings but just so much as to bear them up, and suffer themselves to go with the wind. So that it must necessarily be that almost all aerial insects, and spiders which live upon them and are made up of them, are at the end of the year swept away into the sea and buried in the ocean, and leave nothing behind them but their eggs for a new stock the next year.

      (Edwards, 6-7)

Harmonies anticipate harmonies. The exuberant recreation of the spiders' deathward life rhymes dearly with Ezra's ecstasies in the death-cell. The swinging filaments write creation on the air. Spider plays at real death and so creates. His is the plain physics of ecstasy: profusion out of stillness, and nothing left behind except the next. Edwards discovered this in facts. And what he called "the Creator" we might also call, in company again with Whitehead, "Creativity" itself.

"Creativity" is the universal of universals characterizing ultimate matter of fact. It is that ultimate principle by which the many, which are the universe disjunctively, become the one actual occasion, which is the universe conjunctively. It lies in the nature of things that the many enter into complex unity.

      (Whitehead, 31)

In Pisa, Pound looked to the nearest available facts, there to find, in a bug's life (Disney vs. the Metaphysicals), poetry going on. Continuous motion confirms an origin which shows forth continuity. "Arachne, che mi porta fortuna, go spin on that tent rope." In Windsor, Massachusetts or in Pisa, spider spins mysteries as a matter of fact. The delighted observer is therefore not confined by the metaphysician's "yes, but," the sense of a sign whose sense is elsewhere. Rather, a Jonathan or an Ezra speaks the daylight words of everyday mystery, the "yes and," always refreshed by seeing more and seeing here.

Le paradis n'est pas artificiel
      ("Canto LXXVI")

The spiders are not gone. There's plenty of poetry uncaged in a cage.

En route from Edwards to Pound, the wild fact of spider's paradisal spin delighted Whitman too. If Heaven is no artifice, neither is the soul. But it *is* artful.

> A noiseless patient spider,
> I mark'd where on a little promontory it stood isolated,
> Mark'd how to explore the vacant vast surrounding,
> It launch'd forth filament, filament, filament, out of itself,
> Ever unreeling them, ever tirelessly speeding them.
>
> And you O my soul where you stand,
> Surrounded, detached, in measureless oceans of space,
> Ceaselessly musing, venturing, throwing, seeking the spheres to connect them,
> Till the bridge you will need be form'd, till the ductile anchor hold,
> Till the gossamer thread you fling catch somewhere, O my soul.
> ("A Noiseless Patient Spider")

Adventuring its interiority outward, spider finds itself attached to the real world's space. In Whitman's gaze, it fills a self-made parable of soul. Paradise is the substance of outside, and soul, "launch'd forth," wins objective immortality there. (I cannot help but ask you: do you remember Olson's wonderful passage from "Maximus, at the Harbor?" It goes "Paradise is a person. Come into this world.") Ecstasy escapes to the world. It secures eternity, attaching itself while old forms perish along a thread. Here, the verb "perish" is Whitehead's. (Early in *The Maximus Poems*, in "Maximus, to himself," do you remember, Olson averred that Whitehead had given him "the world?") The gospel of the verb is Whitman's and Whitehead's all at once. And everyone's.

> Forms suffer changing relations; actual entities "perpetually perish" subjectively, but are immortal objectively.
> (Whitehead, 44)

All's well as far as we can feel ourselves attached to it. This is, I'm sure, more of the good luck ("fortune") brought to Pound in Pisa, fortune he would one day, after the prison years were done, catch in a late passage:

> That the body is inside the soul—
> > the lifting and folding brightness
> > > the darkness shattered,
> > > > the fragment.
> ("Canto CXIII")

To stay alive, I only need to stride or to swing inside my soul, because my soul is of the world. My soul is something I saw spinning out of control, re-established as the sweet authority of fact. In Pisa, an *envoi*, and old injunction, gave way to a better one. "Go, little book" became "go spin."

> Arachne, che mi porta fortuna, go spin on that tent rope

We awaken to many connections, the complex unity of our souls as we move towards them, into the day. My dream about Ezra Pound was a delighted overflux, instructing me. Creativity (which I have long since chosen to call "poetry" here at home) continues as the first fact in a continuous sequence. Ecstasy is a way to matter, waking and sleeping. It perishes along a filament of days which never breaks until death, which, objectively speaking, never really happens. Such is the story of "exuberant goodness" a spider told to Jonathan Edwards in 1723. Such is the sermon Whitman heard in a spider's quietness. And such is the good news of material heavens a spider

> Arachne, che mi porta fortuna, go spin on that tent rope

and a butterfly

> Arachne che mi porta fortuna;
> > Athene, who wrongs thee?
> > who wrongs?
> That butterfly has gone out through my smoke hole
> > ("Canto LXXVI")

52

and an ant

        mint springs up again
                in spite of Jones' rodents
        as had the clover by the gorilla cage
                with a four leaf

        When the mind swings by a grass-blade
                an ant's forefoot shall save you
        the clover leaf smells and tastes as its flower
                ("Canto LXXXIII")

brought to an old man to begin his greatest poems in the mind' eye, in
a death cell in which he did not die. Pound was more than consoled by
the heavenly bugs. He was revived with a certainty, as we may be. And
sometimes it is delightful to give that certainty a name. Whitehead
chooses a good one.

        It is termed "God"; because the contemplation of our natures,
        as enjoying real feelings derived from the timeless source of
        all order, acquires that "subjective form" of refreshment and
        companionship at which religions aim.
                (Whitehead, 47)

Refreshment and companionship spin the world. We're getting there.
Poetry is making progress even now.

Works Cited

Jonathan Edwards. *A Jonathan Edwards Reader*, eds. John E. Smith, Harry S. Stout, and Kenneth P. Minkema. New Haven: Yale University Press, 1995.

Charles Olson. *The Maximus Poems*, ed. George F. Butterick. Berkeley: University of California Press, 1983.

Ezra Pound. *The Cantos of Ezra Pound*. New York: New Directions, 1970.

Henry David Thoreau. *Henry David Thoreau*, ed. Robert Sayre. New York: Literary Classics of the United States, 1985.

Alfred North Whitehead. *Process and Reality*. New York: The Macmillan Company, 1929.

Walt Whitman. *Complete Poetry and Collected Prose*, ed Justin Kaplan. New York: Literary Classics of the United States, 1982.

V

A bliss began to happen somewhere. There was America. There was need of America, of an ecstasy whose earth would remain unstolen by a soul. Are we Americans? I ask because I believe all poets everywhere to be Americans in the necessity and abandoned stewardship of bliss. A poem's ambition rests with earth. ("Language is fossil poetry," said Emerson, remember? Buried or exposed, the fossil rests. A poem rests. Only poetry, the ambition of the earth itself, rives on.) And so, in the just governments our poetry conceives, geography is peace, and geography is the guardian of joys. We are (were) Americans only so long as our poems show(ed) non-aggressive expansions of this peace. Manifest Destiny unconfines not nations but rivers and mountains. And the rivers and mountains in their turn more tenderly confine us to grander scales of joy. Thoreau walked a very long time to test the mercy of geography, and he found its limits beyond all measurement, and serene.

> I trust that we shall be more imaginative, that our thoughts will be clearer, fresher, and more ethereal, as our sky – our understanding more comprehensive and broader, like our plains – our intellect generally on a grander scale, like our thunder and lightning, our rivers and mountains and forests – and our hearts shall even correspond in breadth and depth and grandeur to our inland seas. Perchance there will appear to the traveler something, he knows not what, of *laeta* and *glabra*, of joyous and serene, in our very faces. Else to what end does the world go on, and why was America discovered?
> ("Walking," 238)

Whenever it is discovered (and the discovery involves poetry), America finds itself increased by new surroundings. Geography works its wild, wild peace from the outside in. The work is poetry. The poem, non-aggressive even so far as the end of the world, resounds and rests.

And even before Thoreau went walking, a founding father, Jefferson, descried a dynamic peace at work in the confines of his native country. His *Notes on the State of Virginia* declare the sweet dependency of Vision upon geography, declaring also the ways in which geography really acts to rile and then to rest our views. A great passage from "Query IV. A Notice of its Mountains" shows these actions plain.

> The passage of the Potomac through the Blue Ridge is, perhaps, one of the most stupendous scenes in nature. You stand on a very high point of land. On your right comes up the Shenandoah, having ranged along the foot of the mountain an hundred miles to seek a vent. On your left approaches the Potomac, in quest of a passage also. In the moment of their junction, they rush together against the mountain, rend it asunder, and pass off to the sea. The first glance of this scene hurries our senses into the opinion, that this earth has been created in time, that the mountains were formed first, that the rivers began to flow afterwards, that in this place particularly, they have been dammed up by the Blue Ridge of mountains, and have formed an ocean which filled the whole valley; that continuing to rise they have at length broken over at this spot, and have torn the mountain down from its summit to its base. The piles of rock on each hand, but particularly on the Shenandoah, the evident marks of their disrupture and avulsion from their beds by the most powerful agents of nature, corroborate the impression. But the distant finishing which nature has given to the picture, is of a very different character. It is a true contrast to the foreground. It is as placid and delightful as that is wild and tremendous. For the mountain being cloven asunder, she presents to your eye, through the cleft, a small catch of smooth blue horizon, at an infinite distance in the plain country, inviting you, as it were, from the riot and tumult rearing around, to pass through the breach and participate of the calm below. Here the eye ultimately composes itself; and that way, too, the road happens actually to lead.
>
> (182)

Jefferson, the figure and fact of a poet here, is seen to "stand." It is the Shenandoah that "comes up" to him, itself already having widely "ranged." And as the Shenandoah "seek(s)," so the Potomac "quest(s)."

The waters work, and Jefferson is exalted stilly in his place. His very senses are hurried by force of earth and not by any effort of his own. They arrive in good and easy time to see "the distant finishing which nature has given to the picture." Geography's self-evident imagination composes a wild peace in which Jefferson may safely praise and in whose dynamic confines of "riot and tumult" he safely moves. He passes through. The peace keeps him. Great masses and massive forces invite his eye to "calm." Here is ecstasy *in* place and *of* it. Here is exaltation freely given, and expansion of soul involving neither force of will nor act of aggression. Elisa New, in her beautiful study *The Line's Eye* rightly finds an *ars poetica*, a *pax poetica* here.

> This paragraph from "Query IV" makes human will a function of natural fullness, differentiated from that fullness in experience but not strictly in essence. The river's importunities resolve in the smooth sky their movement reflects, and the overall design of the scene makes present urgency, or will, a temporary state that the broadness of experience cycles back into its profounder depths. What Jefferson reveals is an expansive containment, like the Psalmist's image of a cup running over.
>
> (77)

Will dissolves into the wider authority of World. Likewise, human force is obviated by "natural fullness." What New so wisely calls "expansive containment" describes as well a model of American ecstasy, a method of American poetic peace. All transpires by grace and under the guardianship of real geography. On a free Earth, "perception…finds a sweet socket of its relatedness" (New 78). Vision leads the harmless eye to Visionary peace, right here, right now. America at peace is the only real America.

I am writing in early October 2001, and a terrible violence has seized the American eye. Imaginations make wars in Central Asia and mad menaces at home. And so I'm looking for America. I want to find a contemporary eye for peace and a practice of Vision characterized by what Denise Levertov once called (in "Life at War") "the quickness, the sureness, / the deep intelligence living at peace would have." Jefferson gives me the Model and models a Way. And thanks to Elisa New's sweet notion of "expansive containment," I have a test for these in poetry, the place I want to matter. Because it must be an American place, one will of course mean many. I'll choose John Ashbery.

The experimental insouciance of Ashbery's poetry has often distracted readers, myself included, from its fundamental simplicity. Ashbery's is a quiet voice sounded inside worlds it knows and shows to be majestically prolific. Action rests with those worlds, and all his authority derives from the limits they expand within his sight. Thus is Ashbery a true Jeffersonian, and so have his geographies ever described American landscapes of real peace. In "Soonest Mended," his first explicit declaration of dependence, Ashbery made his purpose plain.

> To step free at last, miniscule on the gigantic plateau—
> This was our ambition: to be small and clear and free.
> (*The Double Dream of Spring*, 17)

Freedom rests in an enormous surround. Good poems evidence a clarity of purpose, backgrounded on a grand and moving scale by Earth whose purpose is our home. Like Jefferson, Ashbery finds himself at sites of revelation, there to find forces much greater than but guardian to his own. As the future president was borne up, the latter-day poet is "borne on."

> The clarity of the rules dawned on you for the first time.
> They were the players, and we who had struggled at the game
> Were merely spectators, though subject to its vicissitudes
> And moving with it out of the tearful stadium, borne on
> shoulders, at last.
> Night after night this message returns, repeated
> In the flickering bulbs of the sky, raised past us, taken away
> from us,
> Yet ours over and over until the end that is past truth,
> The being of our sentences, in the climate that fostered them,
> Not ours to own, like a book, but to be with, and sometimes
> To be without, alone and desperate.
> But the fantasy makes it ours, a kind of fence-sitting
> Raised to the level of an esthetic ideal.
> (18)

To the spectator are all spectacles displayed. Sentences of a wild climate, translated onto human scale, become calm, "a kind of fence-sitting / Raised to the level of an esthetic ideal." Call it the impassive passive, a continental peace. Nothing in this place is "ours to own," and yet the mercy of geography underwrites imagination, and imagination "makes it ours." Once again, Earth's purpose is our home.

It has been Ashbery's genius almost effortlessly to map the liberal expanse of nature's sovereignty – i.e. the imagination – upon which human fantasy conducts its peaceful play. Leveled, poetry is raised. (This is democracy in action.) Earth and the poetry of earth show equal justice in expanse and containment.

> And you see, both of us were right, though nothing
> Has somehow come to nothing; the avatars
> Of our conforming to the rules and living
> Around the home have made –well, in a sense, "good citizens"
> of us,
> Brushing the teeth and all that, and learning to accept
> The charity of the hard moments as they are doled out,
> For this is action, this not being sure, this careless
> Preparing, sowing the seeds crooked in the furrow,
> Making ready to forget, and always coming back
> To the mooring of starting out, that day so long ago.
> (19)

I think of William Blake's Clod of Clay: "I ponder, and I cannot ponder; yet I live and love." Thus early in a masterly career, John Ashbery ordered the broad way of human limits towards its brightest flow. Uncertainty moves within a certain sequence, and the arts of peace – "Preparing, sowing the seeds crooked in the furrow" – prove the mystery of that sequence even as they master, by "making ready to forget," the limits it secures.

In peacetime, sequence is both dynamic and secure, a motive force for trust. And it was via trust that Ashbery entered the major phase of his writing life, continuing still. Trust dispenses with sorrow. It ends the conflicts memory, usually in the form of aggressively misremembered claims, sustains against our better natures. In "The New Spirit," Ashbery finds a quiet name for Elisa New's "expansive

61

containment." Too, he entitles Thomas Jefferson's "small catch of smooth blue horizon." It is happiness.

> Are you sad about something today? On days like this the old flanking motion almost seems to be possible again. Certainly the whiff of nostalgia in the air is more than a hint, a glaring proof that the old irregular way of doing is not only some piece of furniture of the memory but is ours, if we had the initiative to use it. I have lost mine. It has been replaced by a strange kind of happiness within the limitations. The way is narrow but it is not hard, it seems almost to propel or push one along. One gets the narrowness into one's seeing, which also seems an inducement to moving forward into what one has already caught a glimpse of and which quickly becomes vision, in the visionary sense, except that in place of the panorama that used to be our customary setting and which we never made much use of, a limited but infinitely free space has established itself, useful as everyday life but transfigured so that its signs of wear no longer appear as a reproach but as indications of how beautiful a thing must have been to have been so much prized, and its noble aspect which must have been irksome before has now become interesting, you are fascinated and keep on studying it. We have broken through into the consequences of the grey, sagging flesh that was our due, and it is surface enchantment, healing to the eye and to the touch.
> (*Three Poems*, 27)

As Jefferson was hurried, so is Ashbery "propel(led)." "Glimpse," contained but moving forward – the dynamic sequence! – "quickly becomes vision." And Vision establishes its further peace. In "a limited but infinitely free space" limitation is no reproach. Earth suffices and then more than suffices as it goes about its daily task of transfiguration. Rivers rend mountains asunder. Our irksome, misremembering will to power is quieted where quiet is ennobled. Vision enchants this surface world even as it heals the eye. And what the eye goes on to see is peace.

Ashbery describes this spectacular event of quietude in a later poem, "On the Towpath" from *Houseboat Days*.

If the thirst would subside just for awhile
It would be a little bit, enough.
This has happened.
The insipid chiming of the seconds
Has given way to an arc of silence
So old it had never ceased to exist
On the roofs of buildings, in the sky.
(22)

As the will subsides, the world proves wide. Where they myth of man-as-measure ends, "an arc of silence" roofs a peaceful earth. Under rigor of the spectacle, earth shows more than wide enough.

The question has been asked
As though an immense natural bridge had been
Strung across the landscape to any point you wanted.
The ellipse is as aimless as that,
Stretching invisibly into the future so as to reappear
In our present.
(23)

Of the Natural Bridge in Virginia, Jefferson wrote "If the view from the top be painful and intolerable, that from below is delightful in an equal extreme" (186). Such radical humility is a delighted extreme, one that "On the Towpath" finds in native motion, presenting the future to a present which remains at rest. Geography commands dynamic trust. As our Jeffersonian poet avers, the command is peace.

Ashbery has kept faith with earth's commands and keeps it still. Delighted trust in expansive containment has left his poetry open, at all levels of discourse, to the dynamics of peace. Limit is not poverty where limits, in their providence, provide abundant distances. In *Your Name Here*, such tender nearness of expanse resounds with special clarity in "Nobody is Going Anywhere."

I don't understand why you object
to any of this. Personally I am above suspicion.
I live in a crawlup where the mice are rotted,
where midnight tunes absolve the bricklayers
and the ceiling abounds in God's sense.

Something more three-dimensional must be breathed
into action...
     (98)

Here, forces of faith – "I am above suspicion" – and the dynamic work
of peace – "where midnight tunes absolve the bricklayers" – breathe
life and magic into seeming deprivation. And so deprivation suddenly
"abounds." The poet finds "God's sense," creation's sense, at the limits of
his own. And then the limits move. This is the truly magical realism
of environment. Its prospects are peace. Its products are an effortless
affirmation.

The porch is loaded, a question-mark
swings like an earring at the base of your cheek:
stubborn, anxious plain. Air and ice,
those unrelenting fatheads, seem always to be saying,
"This is where we will be living from now on."

In the courtyard a plane tree glistens.

The ship is already far from here, like a ghost ship.
The core of the sermon is always distance, landscape
waiting to be considered, maybe loved a little
eventually. And I do, I do.
     (ibid.)

A glistening plane tree rebukes the "unrelenting fatheads." Everything
remains in place, but nothing is still, nothing is captive. Distance, the
visible motive of eye and earth, brings new landscapes always nearer.
And landscapes are the peace when eye weds earth. "And I do, I do."
So much trust, so much time and forbearance are invested in the bold,

bold word "eventually." And this investment is the most considered and considerable work of Ashbery's art.

It is October 15, 2001. We have stopped taking the newspaper, and this morning my son complained that he was missing the news. I thought of the bombs falling somewhere in his little name, and I opened the window shade. I pointed to the red sunrise reflected on the near Spring Mountains and said "There's the news." And I prayed to believe my words myself. In *Self-Portrait in a Convex Mirror*, John Ashbery offered a poem called "The One Thing that Can Save America." Its final lines remain an anthem of forbearance and a timely forecast of the prospects for peace.

> Its truth is timeless, but its time has still
> Not arrived, telling of danger, and the mostly limited
> Steps that can be taken against danger
> Now and in the future, in cool yards,
> In quiet small houses in the country,
> Our country, in fenced areas, in cool shady streets.
>   (45)

Everything abides the world's time, and its truth is coming on – eventually. For now, there are limits to mend, and in the future, limits too. Our country's peace must find and follow them. Then superabundant energies of peace will fill them to overflowing. Everything rides on this eventual earth. As my dear wife Claudia Keelan has avowed in her poem "Day Book," the American soul is "attached / & adventing." We are here, and something is underway here. If this is America, it must be peace. The rivers and mountains and a glistening plane tree all insist: it must be peace.

Works Cited

John Ashbery. *The Double Dream of Spring*. New York: E.P. Dutton & Co., 1970.

—————. *Three Poems*. New York: The Viking Press, 1972.

—————. *Self-Portrait in a Convex Mirror*. New York: The Viking Press, 1975.

—————. *Houseboat Days*. New York: The Viking Press, 1977.

—————. *Your Name Here*. New York: Farrar, Straus & Giroux, 2000.

Claudia Keelan. "Day Book," in *Gare du Nord*, Vol. 2/2, 1999.

Thomas Jefferson. *The Life and Selected Writings of Thomas Jefferson* (eds. Adrienne Koch and William Peden). New York: Random House, 1993.

Denise Levertov. *Poems 1968-1972*. New York: New Directions, 1987.

Elisa New. *The Line's Eye*. Cambridge, MA.: Harvard University Press, 1998.

Henry David Thoreau. *Henry David Thoreau*, ed. Robert Sayre. New York: Literary Classics of the United States, 1985.

—————. *Collected Essays and Poems*. New York: Literary Classics of the United States, 2001.

VI

A poem is something to do in the meantime – not as a pastime, but as an active preparation (parable of the wise and foolish virgins e.g.) as you and I await Horizon's homecoming. Poetry is horizon, of course, a godly site underway, and a true friend at sundown and in the morning. Prepared in good and alive heart, the poem may speed Horizon just a little or stride to meet it on its way. Walt knew: "I am afoot with my vision." And, via Ezra, Li Po too:

> If you are coming down through the narrows of the river Kiang,
> Please let me know beforehand,
> And I will come out to meet you...
>> ("The River-Merchant's Wife: A Letter")

In the meantime a poem proves a succession of behaviors, and these are bodies shown by motion, meaning motion over time. The metaphysics are entirely physical. Blossom is a branch's miraculous horizon, a poetry that glories it, just as sunrise glories those prudent mountains east of me. Branch and mountain are busy. Each prepares in every direction – there are 360 degrees of horizon – for a brightness underway.

So preparation is a behavior whose first motion instantly pluralizes itself. Writing for Horizon, we do not write ourselves into corners but towards eternity ("The authors are in Eternity" – Wm Blake) whose body is numberless. A line prepares for the next line which is likely more than one. Take, for example, William's great poem "Young Sycamore."

> I must tell you
> this young tree
> whose round and firm trunk
> between the wet

pavement and the gutter

. . . .

...rises
bodily

into the air with
one undulant
thrust half its height—
and then

dividing and waning
sending out
young branches on
all sides—

hung with cocoons
it thins
till nothing is left of it
but two

eccentric knotted
twigs
bending forward
hornlike at the top

Thrust out of itself, the tree becomes itself innumerably. A line acts
even so. Each is a lineament of some further embodiment in real time.
Horizon is Horizon because of where and when it prepares to be next.
Likewise, this sycamore shows itself on a line. Then it's sped, preparing
towards an eternity of white space already inscribed, already fleshed by
two twigs.

Poem prepares for poetry. In the sycamore, earth prepares for
air. Such brightening is not bodiless, but a succession of bodies. The
really metaphysical poem – i.e. something of use Here, of use Now as
soul-making and soul-moving – concerns neither objects nor conceits.
It is no reliquary. It is no "bracelet of bright hair about the bone." Its
business is change in all directions which are one Horizon, continuing:
a body departed; a body only now arriving.

that the body of light come forth
                from the body of fire
And that your eyes come to the surface
                from the deep wherein they were sunken,
Reina – for 300 years,
                and now sunken
That your eyes come forth from their caves
                & light then
                        as the holly-leaf
                qui laborat, orat
        (Ezra Pound, from "Canto XCI")

Flesh of fire prepares for flesh of light, right here at the surface. In the poem, this surface is a line, a preparation inclined towards surfaces more perfectly present. Fleshly and sharp for cutting, as metaphysical as the edge of a holly-leaf where it meets the air. "Qui laborat, orat." The work is prayer. It is a presence addressed to something near and answering very closely.

I mean this literally. It is nothing ghostly, just as nothing ghostly happened the other night – January 7, 2002 – to me. It was the first night of the new semester, starry-cold and clear in Salt Lake City. I had an hour to spend before my poetry workshop, and so I walked across the campus, ending up at the library. I went inside to look at magazines. Inside *The Nation*, I found a poem called "Forever" by Shahid Ali who'd died exactly one month prior to the night I'm writing about. The poem was dedicated to me, and I'd not known my friend had written it. Suddenly, the question of eternity was very much a physical fact at hand – like the cold outside, and the starry sky, and the lighted room full of younger poets across the quad waiting for me and for Shahid and, whether they believed in it or not, for eternity.

Even Death won't hide the poor fugitive forever...

The nightwork before me would be a prayer addressed to them, just as Shahid's "Forever" was and remains an answer underway to my busy waiting. It is very real presences poems prepare, and new bodies, nearly. Forever, like the edge of a leaf and the latest news from the dead and all such horizons, is never more of the same.

The horizon of eternity dotes upon substance, and so the soul prepares substantialness. Eliot oughtn't to have been ironic. Our metaphysics *are* warm, being physical from the first (e.g. it was a particular and a cold night, and then and there did Shahid's poem happen to me) and being occupied early with eternity. In a poem called "My Spirit," Thomas Traherne puts this occupation forward as the first substance and first behavior of a simply naked I.

> My naked simple life was I.
> That act so strongly shin'd
> Upon the earth, the sea, the sky,
> It was the substance of my mind.
> The sense itself was I.
> I felt no dross nor matter in my soul,
> No brims nor borders, such as in a bowl
> We see, my essence was capacity
> That felt all things,
> The thought that springs
> Therefrom's itself. It hath no other wings
> To spread abroad, nor eyes to see,
> Nor hands distinct to feel,
> Nor knees to kneel:
> But being simple like the Deity
> In its own centre is a sphere
> Not shut up here, but everywhere.

Life is act. Mind is substance, and our sense, those living conduits of Horizon, shape selves and souls whose "essence" is "capacity," a fact prepared to be filled. We are sites where soul is sighted. And a poem is likewise a volume (but not a vacuum) made for poetry. The eye opens, and only *then* is it an organ of vision. The poem opens, and only *then* comes poetry. The eye and the clean page are simples, like the simpleness of God, making places for their own. But never their own until the place is made, until, as Traherne says later, "essence is transformed into a True / And perfect act." Bodies build the fires where metaphysics glow.

But yet of this I was most sure,
　　That at the utmost length
　　(So worthy was it to endure),
　　My soul could best express its strength.
　　It was so quick and pure,
That all my mind was wholly everywhere,
Whate'er it saw, 'twas ever wholly there;
The sun ten thousand legions off, was nigh:
　　　The utmost star,
　　　Tho seen from far,
Was present in the apple of my eye.
　　There was my sight, my life, my sense,
　　　My substance and my mind.
　　　My spirit shin'd
Even there, not by transeunt influence.
　　The act was immanent, yet there.
　　The thing remote, yet felt even here.

Horizon speeds to the opened eye at light-speed. Instantly, the ready
poem is poetry. Expression? Expression is purely a distance seen to
close.

　　From all direction, transformations close upon the opened eye, and
the eye is transformed. Nothing is more wildly formal or more physical
than this momentous change. So for the eye, and for the poem also,
preparation changes the nature of waiting into action. Metaphysics
bursts the chrysalis of metaphor. In the 3rd century, Plotinus made a
dictum for the brightness underway.

> No eye that has not become like unto the sun will ever look
> upon the sun; nor will any that is not beautiful look upon the
> beautiful. Let each one therefore become godlike and beautiful
> who would contemplate the divine and beautiful.
> (The Essential Plotinus, 43)

The opening eye becomes like light. Opening, the poem whose
imagination inclines to change utterly – new cadences, new twigs,
fires and substances and no conceits – becomes more and more like
poetry. At such a moment, Horizon walks and talks with you and me.

(I suddenly remember Walt again – "The sea whisper'd me." Was any child ever so busily prepared, ever so wildly rocked as he?)

In company with Horizon, a poem moves effortlessly and everywhere. We do not strain after sunshine. And in such union, our preparations win to vivid transformations. There's no more work to do. In *The Book of the Green Man*, Ronald Johnson opens his eyes and finds himself exactly so.

> I find I advance with
> sidereal motions
> —my eyes containing substance
>
> of the sun,
> my ears built of beaks and feathers—
>
> I ascend with saps
>
> & flower in season
>
> & eddy with tides.
>
>
> With every moon,
> I come from the darkness into incandescence.
>
> My tongue assumes the apple's flesh
> & my skin the infinite spheres of the thistle's prickle. And as I breathe
>
> the wind has its billow — & all the grasses —
>
> in a combing, mazy movement.
>   (from "Emanations")

Amazement is a way of life where the attentions rive, "in a combing, mazy movement," masses into ways. Johnson shows this on the language of his own attendant flesh. Metaphysics breaks into the open, wearing skins.

So light inscribes, and what Pound called "the body of light" proves the inscriptions, just as Horizon shows a sunrise, and poetry, sometimes, proves the poems native to our words.

Today I saw the word written on the poplar leaves.

It was "dazzle". *The dazzle of the poplars.*

As a leaf startles out

from an undifferentiated mass of foliage,

so the word did from a leaf—

(from "What the Leaf Told Me")

"Dazzle" was written without effort. "Dazzle" was read without effort. The poet's preparation says "Today I saw." The rest is a matter of course, like the world's turning. I cannot help but remember a moment near the end of *Under the Volcano*:

> The Consul laughed: just to glance at him was to feel that mankind was on the point of being saved immediately. He repeated the good Mexican joke, not quite right, in English, patting the policeman, whose jaw had dropped in bewilderment and who was eyeing him blankly, on the arm. "I learn that the world goes round so I am waiting here for my house to pass by." He held out his hand. "Amigo," he said.
> (355)

"Amigo" also means "afoot with my vision," and, too, it means Horizon, the experimental companion for whom Coleridge named his magazine "The Friend." No wonder the policeman was bewildered. Laws can never apprehend Horizon.

Of all contemporary poets, it is Robin Blaser who has entered upon the most sustained and soul-making preparations for poetry's Horizon.

In tender epic, *The Holy Forest*, he time and again has moved the speech of conversation and prayer to visionary stride. (Read it!) Consequently, great things make their way into his eyes. Here, for one example, is an amazing passage from "Image-Nation 7 (l'air:"

actual

thinkable things   cling
to the unthinkable

two-fold   folds   like a
beloved   o laughter
beside my path

companions   are horizons
obsessions of snow, pearl
flower shape stone fire scenery
marrow of white elder, virgin wax
and sperm at last closes the circle

spiritual plain coach of fire
window of flesh road of souls
wombs of coals breasts of flames
husbands of virgins beard of God

laughter preparations,   *naivetes*
flames frost,   *cutting off*
reparations leveling
inexpressible purity

whirlwind of souls white atoms
here we are again at a landscape
burning silver mage's souls
stolen stars flying spirits

sharp sighs greedy lips
sweet conflagration
purified lily snow of years

and this

     wheel

          turns into

     ecstasy

heart-shaped stone heart   in a box
Chinese box of deer feeding at the flowering gate
love lasts
a world
    covering
his eyes   the glory
of the sea   disappears
shining   into the eye
           (*The Holy Forest*, 122-123)

Delighted conflagrations hasten from every direction here, conjoining in the unsurpassed peace of a poem (and eye) to which poetry has lordly and lovingly come – "Chinese box of deer feeding at the flowering gate." A poem is something to do in the meantime. At light-speed, the meantime flowers peacefully for as far as eternity – "purified lily snow of years" – goes.

Works Cited

Agha Shahid Ali. "Forever" in *The Nation*, January 7/14, 2002, page 52.

Robin Blaser. *The Holy Forest*. Toronto: Coach House Press, 1993.

Ronald Johnson. *The Book of the Green Man*. New York: W.W. Norton & Co., 1967.

Malcolm Lowry. *Under the Volcano*. New York: J.P. Lippincott, 1947.

Plotinus. *The Essential Plotinus*, ed. Elmer O'Brien, S. J. Indianapolis: Hackett Publishing Company, Inc., 1964.

Ezra Pound. *The Cantos of Ezra Pound*. New York: New Directions, 1970.

Henry David Thoreau. *Henry David Thoreau*, ed. Robert Sayre. New York: Literary Classics of the United States, 1985.

Thomas Traherne. *Selected Poems and Prose*, ed. Alan Bradford. London: Penguin Books, 1991.

William Carlos Williams. *Selected Poems*, ed. Charles Tomlinson. New York: New Directions, 1985.

VII

I'm writing in early May 2002, white sweet May. There's a bird on the clothesline. My five new locust trees are too tender to bear his weight just yet. I'm tired. A good but difficult year of teaching and traveling has ended, and I'm happy to be home. I live not far to the southwest of Las Vegas, a city that is, among so many other things, sweet haven for the broken ecstatic: a city where, to paraphrase Ezra, the gondolas cost too much *every* year, but it's a pleasure to see them all under one big roof. I've written a lot about means and measures of ecstasy – its incandescent demands and clamor, its swing towards new flesh finally alone. But as I say, I'm tired and glad to have Las Vegas nearby. I'm glad for its unspoken and unexpiring offer of ecstasies at second-hand.

At Treasure Island hotel & casino, Cirque du Soleil does a beautiful show called *Mystère*. I was skeptical at first, having only vague and seedy memories of circuses I'd seen as a child. But good friends invited me, and so I went. Once the show began, once the extravagant performers took to the air, I started to smile, and I smiled for nearly two hours. A tired man loves a circus. A tired ecstasy is grateful to shut its inward eye and wake to spectacle. The dazzle of other human bodies wheeling and capering refreshes a body at rest, and after a while, excess might mean access once again. As Charles Ives wrote in his song "The Circus Band," "Ain't it a grand and glorious noise!" (Joyful, too, the way God likes it. Our ecstasy is God's circus after all.)

While I watched the Cirque du Soleil, I lived moments breathtaking not from danger but from joy. I felt the tug of transcendence not as a risk, but as a smile. (Oh please, let us never talk about "risk" in poetry! Let's have fun.) Seeing perfections sustained above empty air, I borrowed conviction from their flamboyance. Deathlessness at second-hand felt deathless all the same. Ives' song for the circus ends

> Where is the lady all in pink?
> She waved to me last year I think.
> Can she have died? Can! that! rot!
> She is passing but she sees me not.

Ives' exclamations shout defiance to death. Circus shouts refresh our words. (How wonderfully the ladies shouted on the trapezes at Treasure Island above and beyond me!) I want to write a while about the poetry of circuses.

Performance transforms a place into an occasion. A poem, let's say, takes place when words burst out of customary mind. And a circus happens where and whenever some tatterdemalion body discards itself in leaps and somersaults. Poetry outspeeds language. In his moment, the acrobat outreaches his own skin. Rilke, a student of saltimbanques on canvas (Picasso's) and on street corners (Paris'), understood the edge of acrobatics and all its transcendent pang.

> In front of the Luxembourg Gardens, near the Pantheon,
> Père Rollin and his Troupe have spread themselves out again.
> The same carpet is lying there, the same coats, thick winter
> overcoats, taken off and piled on top of a chair, leaving just
> enough room for the little boy, the old man's grandson, to come
> and sit down now and then during breaks. He still needs to,
> he is still just a beginner, and those headlong leaps out of high
> somersaults down onto the ground make his feet ache. He has
> a large face that can contain a great many tears, but sometimes
> they stand in his widened eyes almost out to the edge. Then he
> has to carry his head cautiously, like a too-full cup. It's not that
> he is sad, not at all; he wouldn't even notice it if he were; it is
> simply the pain that is crying, and he has to let it cry. In time it
> gets easier and finally it goes away...
> (from "Acrobats," trans. Stephen Mitchell)

On a winter street between gardens and gods, winter is discarded like an overcoat. A circus springs. And city life becomes circus life because of carpets and a chair. Rilke's scene is a chrysalis of itself, shed as the boy sheds his tears and, finally, his pain. The acrobat, human filled with something beyond humanness, simply overflows. Like poetry, a circus is a deluge.

In another part of Paris and on a different day (July 13, 1913) Guillaume Apollinaire happened upon a sudden circus of his own. In "Phantom of Clouds," street and carpet and tatterdemalion likewise occasion an overflux of change. The poem ends:

They decided to begin the performance
From beneath the organ appeared a tiny juggler dressed in
pulmonary pink
With fur at his wrist and ankles
He gave little cries
And saluted by gracefully lifting his forearms
And spreading wide his fingers

One leg back ready to kneel
He saluted the four points of the compass
And when he balanced on a sphere
His thin body became such delicate music that none of the
onlookers could resist it
A small inhuman sprite
Each of them thought
And that music of shapes
Destroyed the music of the mechanical organ
That the man with the ancestor-covered face was grinding out

The tiny juggler turned cartwheels
With such harmony
That the organ stopped playing
And the organist hid his face in his hands
His fingers resembled descendants of his destiny
Miniscule fetuses appearing in his beard
New cries like Redskins
Angelic music of the trees
Vanishing of the child

The jugglers raised the huge dumbbells at arm's length
They juggled with weights
But every spectator searched in himself for the miraculous
child
Century oh century of clouds
       (trans. Anne Hyde Greet)

The "tiny juggler" gracefully annihilates everything: time and space,
music and shape. All "four points of the compass" are refreshed and

entertained by catastrophe. Supra-humanness inundates the street and then it vanishes. Like poetry, a circus disappears. (Think of the final shot in Charlie Chaplin's "The Circus," that circle in the dust.) What it leaves behind is a new species of silence, a "miraculous child" in the air and in ourselves.

In his finest work, D.H. Lawrence imagines a new species of human birth and better directions out of childhood than History, Society, and the frightened discourse of Modern Life. In poems collected as *Pansies* (hardy little flowers of outrage, "pensees" strewn by the wayside), this imagination clowns and opines in sharpest earnest. "When I Went to the Circus" describes an elemental strife under the big top. Amid colors and animals, delight struggles to be born.

> The tight-rope lady, pink and blonde and nude-looking,
>   with a few gold spangles
> footed cautiously out on the rope, turned prettily, spun
>   round
> bowed, and lifted her foot in her hand, smiled, swung her
>   parasol
> to another balance, tripped round, poised, and slowly sank
> her handsome thighs down, down, till she slept her
>   splendid body on the rope.
> When she rose, tilting her parasol, and smiled at the
>   cautious people
> they cheered, but nervously.
>
> The trapeze man, slim and beautiful and like a fish in the
>   air
> swung great curves through the upper space, and came
>   down like a star
> --And the people applauded, with hollow, frightened applause.

The perilous, happy eros of the tightrope-lady makes the audience cringe, even as they cheer. And the trapeze man, a mythological creature, part fish, part meteor, simply terrifies them. Lawrence sees bright coupling in the air and an ecstasy which the ground will not accept. The miraculous child of tightrope and trapeze remains unborn, remains nearly unimaginable. Modernity is a discourse, and circus life

84

and circus miracles make no parley. Clowns shriek. Acrobats exclaim.
They don't talk, and animals roar and trumpet behind them. "Ain't it
a grand and glorious noise!" The circus, as Lawrence shows, is, for the
most part, alone with itself – just as poetry is alone with language, just
as any true worshipper is alone with the Alone.

> When modern people see the carnal body dauntless and
>   flickering gay
> playing among the elements neatly, beyond competition
> and displaying no personality,
> modern people are depressed.
> Modern people feel themselves at a disadvantage.
> They know they have no bodies that could play among the
>   elements.
>
> They have only their personalities, that are best seen flat,
>   on the film,
> flat personalities in two dimensions, imponderable and
>   touchless.
>
> And they grudge the circus people the swooping gay
>   weight of limbs
> that flower in mere movement,
> and they grudge them the immediate, physical understanding
> they have with their circus beasts,
> and they grudge them their circus-life altogether.
>
> Yet the strange, almost frightened shout of delight that
>   comes now and then from the children
> shows that the children vaguely know how cheated they
>   are of their birthright
> in the bright wild circus flesh.

Here too, as for Rilke and Apollinaire, the circus is a body full to
bursting, a flesh at the point of flowering into something new. Yet only
the children's intermittent shouting (circus shouts refresh our words)
is anywise aware. A birthright swings out of reach. The "bright wild

85

circus flesh" is glimpsed, then gone. Like poetry, a circus disappears. And birth is a disappearance too.

It's strange and somehow right that, in the matter of circuses, rebirth and regret, transcendence and abandonment should be so intertwined. Becoming a poem, the glorious noise lapses into language. Becoming the trapeze-artist, a mythical beast slips into tights. Circus shouts refresh our words, but after the din dies down, the words are words again. No poet has more tenderly expressed this bittersweetness than Kenneth Koch. The very first lines of his now-classic "The Circus" say it plainly: "We will have to go away, said the girls in the circus / And never come back anymore." A circus comes and goes. Does it ever return? Koch catastrophizes the narrative hidden in Charles Ives' little song ("Can she have died" Can! that! rot!") and shows catastrophe to be a circus truth – evanescent and eternal all at once.

> Suddenly a great scream breaks out in the circus tent!
> It is Aileen the trapeze artist, she has fallen into the dust and dirt
> From so high! She must be dead! The stretcher bearers rush out,
> They see her lovely human form clothed in red and white and orange wiry net,
> And they see that she does not breathe anymore.
> The circus doctor leaves his tent, he runs out to care for Aileen.
> He traverses the circus grounds and the dusty floor of the circus entrance, and he comes
> Where she is, now she has begun to move again, she is not dead,
> But the doctor tells her he does not know if she will ever be able to perform on the trapeze again,
> And he sees the beautiful orange and red and white form shaken with sobs,
> And he puts his hand on her forehead and tells her she must lie still.
>
> The circus girls form a cortege, they stand in file in the yellow and white sunlight.
> "What is death in the circus? That depends on if it is spring

Then, if elephants are there, *mon père*, we are not completely
lost.
Oh the sweet strong odor of beasts which laugh at decay!
Decay! decay! We are like the elements in a kaleidoscope,
But such passions we feel! bigger than beaches and
Rustier than harpoons." After his speech the circus practitioner
sat down.
("The Circus," stanzas 8 & 9)

There is a scream and a flamboyant commotion. Quickly pleasure
couples with pain, delight with death. Havoc is a certain circus-joy,
a gravitas tugging us not downward, but every which way. And after
the scream comes speech. The circus doctor (the figure of a poet if
ever there was one; Yeats would know) articulates the sweet and rotten
intertwinements, the rust and enormity circus life upholds. And then
the doctor sits down.

Koch's circus is the poem of a circus with its trajectories all on
show. The scream is a zenith; its consequence is a slow descent.
Beginning in crazy parade, a circus ends as a cortege. And when it is
gone, the world is alone with itself again.

The circus doctor stood beside the lake. In his hand he held a
black briefcase.
A wind ruffled the surface of the lake and slightly rocked the
boats.

Red and green fish swam beneath the surface of the water.
The doctor went into the lunchroom and sat down. No, he
said, he didn't care for anything to eat.
The soft wind of summer blew in the light green trees.
("The Circus," from stanza 12)

Nature, with its actual trees and fish and death, slips in behind the
circus. There is no landscape under the big top, but there is only
landscape after the tents come down.

Where does the circus go when it has gone? Its songs and noise
must still be rising. Its colors must be speeding somewhere as light.
Through muddle and myth and miracle, the poetry of circuses proposes

a physical law: call it the Law of Conservation of Ecstasy. Ecstasy can neither be created nor destroyed. It's constant because it goes. And where it goes is from second to first-hand. Energies know their originality by showing origins, and the Cirque du Soleil is a circle like the sun. The greatest of all circus poets was Robert Lax. In *The Circus of the Sun*, he made a psalmody of jugglers, acrobats and clowns, a book of praises for folk whose every action shows the form of praise.

> They lie in slumber late, the acrobats;
> They sleep and do not know the sun is up.
> Nor does the Lord wake them,
> Nor do the sun's rays touch them.
> And the Lord, who has chosen them,
> The Lord, who created them,
> Leaves them in slumber until it is time.
> Slowly, slowly, His hand is upon the morning's lyre,
> Makes a music in their sleeping.
> And they turn, and turning wonder
> Eyes awake to light of morning.
> They rise, dismounting from their beds,
> They rise and hear the light airs playing
> Songs of praise unto the Lord.
> The circus is a song of praise,
> A song of praise unto the Lord.
> The acrobats, his chosen people,
> Rejoice forever in His love.
> (from "The Morning Stars")

Where does the circus go? It rises. It takes instruction from the sun from which it takes its name. When I am tired, I look up. And if I look, I sometimes see. Sometimes spectacle becomes a vision. Sometimes a circus *is* a sun.

> Rastelli was a juggler and a kind of sun
> His clubs and flames and hoops
> Moved around him like planets
> Obeyed and waited his command

He moved all things according to their natures:
They were ready when he found them
But he moved them according to their love.

As dancers harmonize, the rising falling planets
mirrored his movements.
Rising, falling, rotating, revolving they spun on
the axis of his desire.
Clubs were at rest, he woke them and sent them spinning;
From which again they flew, until flying and falling,
Spinning and standing a moment in mid-air,
They seemed to love to obey his command,
And even dance with the juggler.

Seeing the world was willing to dance,
Rastelli fell in love with creation,
Through the creation with the Creator,
And through the Creator again with creation,
And through the creation, the Lord.

He loved the world and things he juggled,
He loved the people he juggled for.
Clubs and hoops could answer his love:
Even more could people.

Lover and juggler
Bearer of light
He lived and died in the center ring
Dancing decorously
Moving all things according to their nature

And there, before the Lord, he dances still.
      (from "Rastelli")

In such plain cadences, Robert Lax discerns a cosmic law which draws
the juggler upwards to the throne of creation. In the clubs and hoops
we see an extravagant sublime. Nothing made. Nothing destroyed.
Everything sustained. Elsewhere, this would be a pastoral moment.

And somewhere else again (say the island of Patmos), it would be a Revelation. Here, it is a circus act, an empty circle of useless spinning things whose axis is desire and whose excess is ecstasy in its purest form. In a "Postscript" to *The Circus of the Sun*, Robert Lax avows the perfect justice and sublimity of a juggler's extravagance.

> *...In a world of men condemned to earn their bread by the sweat of their brows, the liberty of those who, like the lilies of the field, live by playing. For playing is like Wisdom before the face of the Lord. Their play is praise. Their praise is prayer. This play, like the ritual gestures of the priest, is characterized by grace; Heavenly grace unfolding, flowering and reflected in the physical grace of the player.*
>
> *I had a friend, a Hindu monk named Bramachari, whose monastery near Calcutta was called Sri Angan, which he translated as "The Playground of the Lord." That is the key to the whole matter, the monks playing joyously and decorously before the Lord, praising the Lord. The playground, though sown with tares, is a reflection of Eden. I think there can be a "Circus of the Lord."*

The circus shares in the indispensable uselessness of all saints. When we are weary, we are weary for justice. We are weary for joy. May the circus intercede.

Works Cited

Guillaume Apollinarie. *Calligrammes*, trans. Anne Hyde Greet. Berkeley: University of California Press, 1980.

Charles Ives. *114 Songs*. New York: Associated Music Publishers, Inc., Peer International Corporation, and Theodore Presser Company, 1922.

Kenneth Koch. *Selected Poems*. New York: Random House, 1985.

D.H. Lawrence. *The Complete Poems*. New York: Viking Press, 1971.

Robert Lax. *Love Had a Compass: Journals and Poetry*. New York: Grove Press, 1996.

Rainer Maria Rilke. *Ahead of All Parting: The Selected Poetry and Prose*, trans. Stephen Mitchell. New York: Random House, 1995.

Henry David Thoreau. *Henry David Thoreau*, ed. Robert Sayre. New York: Literary Classics of the United States, 1985.

VIII

*A*lone with the Alone, poetry is nevertheless ringed round by a friendship and by the adventure of Friendship. A poem is a force for change produced by a change, bearing witness to some new phase (or phrase) in the loving relationship between a poet's soul and a poet's self. These friends are a solitude together, and the conversation of their silence leaves a trace, a phosphorescence if you will. The trace is a poem.

I have taken my title for these columns from the "Wednesday" chapter, the great essay on friendship, in Henry Thoreau's *A Week on the Concord and Merrimack Rivers*. But the phrase "invisible green" makes an even earlier appearance, at the very end of his journal entry dated June 11, 1840. There, my author thinks to lay himself down beside his soul, his glow-friend, and begins to know the adventure of time from a more supernal point of view.

> We stole noiselessly down the stream, occasionally driving a pickerel from the covert of the pads – or bream from her nest – and the small green bittern would now and then sail away on sluggish wings from some recess of the Shore. With its patient study by rocks and sandy capes, has it wrested the whole of her secret from nature yet? It has looked out from its dull eye for so long, standing on one leg – on moon and stars sparkling through silence and dark – and now what a rich experience is its – What says it of stagnant pools – and reeds – and damp night fogs? It would be worth while to look in the eye which has been open and seeing at such hours and in such solitudes.
>
> When I behold that dull yellowish green I wonder if my own soul is not a bright invisible green. I would fain lay my eye side by side with its – and learn of it.
>
> (*Journal*, 126)

Birds are the oldest symbols we construe as human souls, largely because of the freedom and impassivity of their aerial perspective. Here, Thoreau projects himself into the symbol's actual eye. The hours and solitudes of "the small green bittern" envisage real shores of slow time with sparkling entirety. And entirety is the Soul the Self wishes to befriend.

The Soul awaits the Self, but very busily, attentive to the world's green work. There in that world, at birth, Self enters a relationship to which it awakens only over time. Soul has been present the whole time, wrapped in the world and rapt with it. Its captivation is a rapture ready to share. Via poems, as via all companionable scripture, Self is sometimes given over to a generous portent of waking. And right there is Soul, rapture to hand, nearest presence of the splendid presentation.

> Whatever is born, Arjuna, whether it moves or it moves
> not, know that it comes from the union of the field and
> the knower of the field.
>
> He who sees that the lord of all is ever the same in all
> that is, immortal in the field of mortality – he sees the truth.
> And when a man sees that the God in himself is the same
> God in all that is, he hurts not himself by hurting others:
> then he goes indeed to the highest Path.
>
> He who sees that all work, everywhere, is only the work
> of nature; and that the Spirit watches this work – he sees
> the truth.
> (*The Bhagavad Gita*, chapter 13, verses 26-29)

In terms of this wisdom, Soul is one knower of the field (in *The Bhagavad Gita*, the field is the cosmos) and knowledge a rapturous union begetting all things, and each. We are the offspring of our friend. (For example, Dante was the superlegitimate son of Virgil, Whitman the superlegitimate child of a hermit-thrush.) Each new phase of Self's relationship to Soul is thus fundamentally original, is birth itself contacting new entireties. There's no effort involved, only waking and the portents of further waking, only the touching of the trace of warm adventure. Adventurous poems show wonderful births. Phosphorescent poems show new lights stirring out of old. The passages (sometimes these are poems) twixt Soul and Self are composed at prolific rest, envisioned by their Vision of themselves entwined, an irresistible providence.

94

A poem begins, then, as the perfect rest, an infinite capacity close by prolific sources. Intending nothing, it is tended to. What did I mean by being born? Nothing. And then the world meant me. In "My Spirit" (I can never let go of this poem), Thomas Traherne offers his own birth as one such stunning election. Emptiness as the beneficiary of All. Soul as an overflux which Self contains resistlessly, i.e. effortlessly.

> My naked simple life was I.
>   That act so strongly shin'd
> Upon the earth, the sea, the sky,
> It was the substance of my mind.
>   The sense itself was I.
> I felt no dross nor matter in my soul,
> No brims nor borders, such as in a bowl
> We see, my essence was capacity.

The "naked simple" act of an I, intending nothing, entrusts its essential capacity to a friend: to Soul and, via Soul, to the world. What do senses do? They entrust themselves. The opened eye is helpless and instantly filled by the available light. Likewise the opened poem. How does a poem begin? It entrusts itself. The splendid presentation then presents the available splendors, right there on the line.

> This made me present evermore
>   With whatsoe'er I saw.
> An object, if it were before
> My eye, was by Dame Nature's law,
>   Within my soul. Her store
> Was all at once within me; all her treasures
> Were my immediate and internal pleasure,
> Substantial joys, which did inform my mind.
>   With all she wrought,
>   My soul was fraught,
> And every object in my heart a thought
>   Begot, or was; I could not tell,
>   Whether the things did there
>   Themselves appear,

Which in my spirit truly seem'd to dwell;
    Or whether my conforming mind
    Were not even all that therein shin'd.

Self conforms to Soul as to a radiance. This has nothing whatsoever to do with submission or with abnegation. The conformity is mutual and progressive. Self provides shapeliness, and Soul, substance. Two providences intertwine and then adventure together. Eyes conform so to light, and light to the seeing eye. Poems conform to matters and meanings instantly their own. As Traherne avows, there's no border to the begettings. Vision is transgression in every direction. The world shines in the poem, and the poem radiates new light and soul-full shapeliness.

         'Twas not a sphere
         Yet did appear
   One infinite. 'Twas somewhat everywhere.
     And tho it had a power to see
      Far more, yet still it shin'd
      And was a mind
  Exerted for it saw infinity.
    'Twas not a sphere, but 'twas a power
    Invisible, and yet a bower.

    Self and Soul are intertwined, not married. A poem and the world may (must) be deeply involved, but are not wed. Radiance is no institution. Traherne's genius and candor resound in the amazing word "somewhat." Capacity and splendor meet "somewhat everywhere." And poems are "exerted" by no exertion of their own. Great powers are at work, and still the occasion is one of perfect rest. A poem is a bower.

    Now occurs to me the near and American instance of all this. (Of course, I always see Traherne, apostle of improved infancy, as an American figure. We'd never have known his poems at all had they not, in the early 1900s, been rescued from the dustman's burn. And as for *The Bhagavad Gita*, well, Henry Thoreau made *that* particular scripture pointedly American a long time ago. He was ever a Hindu missionary unto himself and his friends.) What occurs to me now is that wherever there is an American poet, there are two. The paradigmatic providence of Self and Soul applies exactly at the site of a poem. The lines are interleavings. We read double. So it is that "Song of Myself" very early shows to be "Song *and* Myself."

> Trippers and askers surround me,
> People I meet, the effect upon me of my early life or the
>   ward and city I live in, or the nation,
> The latest dates, discoveries, inventions, societies, authors
>   old and new,
> My dinner, dress, associates, looks, compliments, dues,
> The real or fancied indifference of some man or woman I
>   love,
> The sickness of one of my folks or of myself, or ill-doing
>   or loss or lack of money, or depressions or exaltations,
> Battles, the horrors of fratricidal war, the fever of doubtful
>   news, the fitful events;
> These come to me days and nights and go from me again,
> But they are not the Me myself.
> Apart from the pulling and hauling stands what I am,
> Stands amused, complacent, compassionating, idle, unitary,
> Looks down, is erect, or bends an arm on an impalpable
>   certain rest,
> Looking with side-curved head curious what will come
>   next,
> Both in and out of the game and watching and wondering
>   at it.

> Backward I see in my own days where I sweated through
>   fog with linguists and contenders,
> I have no mocking or arguments, I witness and wait.

The "I am" that stands apart stands so because it "sweated through" the argument of birth. Original energies stir through contention and waken Self. And where Self awakes is a bower: in "Song of Myself," a nuptial bower, to borrow Milton's Edenic phrase. Beyond the noise of mockings and arguments lie Self and Soul imparadised in one another's arms. In a poem's bower, poetry is the embrace.

I believe in you my soul, the other I am must not abase
    itself to you,
And you must not be abased to the other.

Loafe with me on the grass, loose the stop from your
    throat,
Not words, not music or rhyme I want, not custom or lec-
    ture, not even the best,
Only the lull I like, the hum of your valved voice.

I mind how once we lay such a transparent summer
    morning,
How you settled your head athwart my hips and gently
    turn'd over upon me,
And parted the shirt from my bosom-bone, and plunged
    your tongue to my bare-stript heart,
And reach'd till you felt my beard, and reach'd till you
    held my feet.

In "the lull I like," the Whitman who is one and two is laved by
alliterative innocence. This restoration of the poet transpires beyond
words, music, and rhyme. Writers may work. I suppose I'm working
now. But poets rest a procreant rest. Self alone with Soul alone
profuses peace. A heaven here and now and furthering.

Swiftly arose and spread around me the peace and
    knowledge that pass all argument of the earth,
And I know that the hand of God is the promise of my
    own,
And I know that the spirit of God is the brother of my
    own,
And that all the men ever born are also my brothers, and
    the women my sisters and lovers,
 And that a kelson of the creation is love,
And limitless are leaves stiff or drooping in the fields,
And brown ants in the little wells beneath them,
And mossy scabs of the worm fence, heap'd stones, elder,
    mullein and poke-weed.

The peace is uncontrollable: not a poem, but a world; and not another world, but *this* one. The inclusive conjunctions profuse such plain facts as will not be pent in stanzas. In the embrace of Self and Soul, poetry is present at the creation of the world, an instance that happens never to end. And that is why "Song of Myself" never ends. It simply "stop(s) somewhere waiting." For whom? For you and for me. Wonderful that in the original 1855 edition, the poem rests unpunctuated at the end, ready to hand for the next poet, a rapture ready to share. I begin to believe that Whitman is the literal Soul of American poems. He is, as he himself avowed – "I witness and wait"—a Self gone over to Soul, a small green bittern's eye gone all the way over to invisible green. "If you want me again look for me under your bootsoles." Whenever we awake, we stand with Whitman or, if you prefer, upon the soulful ground Walt Whitman has become. In the nuptials of the art, wherever there is one American poet, there are two.

(And only one is none at all.)

In the 20th-century, no American more epically resisted the yawp and lull of *Leaves of Grass* than Ezra Pound. The Idaho Kid, self-exiled to inward Ecbatans, made of one Modernism (the highest of High Modernisms, I would say) a sustained catastrophizing of the bittern's eye and foundling's bower. The paradise of the early *Cantos* is a bejeweled palimpsest, a text made of texts, and very little to do with the greeny substance of Soul's embrace. But then there came the blessed catastrophe at Pisa. Alone with the unlettered grass and insects surrounding his cage at the Detention Center, Pound descried an aloneness freely offered to his own, one more elegant and loving, more handy and substantial, than any he had dreamed. *The Pisan Cantos* show a Vision of the outward eye humbled and beloved by what it sees. In "Canto LXXXI," this Vision is lifted to lowly apogee and procreant climax in stanzas which have since become Pound's signature perfection. Here is the end of combative Modernism in a new birth (and burst) of peace.

> What thou lov'st well remains,
> > the rest is dross
> What thou lov'st well shall not be reft from thee
> What thou lov'st well is thy true heritage
> Whose world, or mine or theirs

> or is it of none?
> First came the seen, then thus the palpable
>   Elysium, though it were in the halls of hell,
> What thou lov'st well is thy true heritage
> What thou lov'st well shall not be reft from thee
>
> The ant's a centaur in his dragon world.
> Pull down thy vanity, it is not man
> Made courage, or made order, or made grace,
>   Pull down thy vanity, I say pull down.
> Learn of the green world what can be thy place
> In scaled invention or true artistry,
> Pull down thy vanity
>   Paquin pull down!
> The green casque has outdone your elegance.

The peace is uncontrollable: not a poem, but a world; and not another world, but *this* one. High fashion (Paquin & Co., Modernism & Co.) is outdistanced and outdone by a "green casque," by the real world's simplest discard. The overthrow is tender. The news is better than ever Ezra could have imagined, because the news is not imaginary. Hourly expecting execution for treason, he is instead imparadised by loves, palpable loves. What happened? Biographies and literary criticism offer many explanations, but it all comes down to this: he looked for something under his bootsoles. And right there, the ground raised up a Soul to be his own, his darling – "What thou lov'st well" – and two. Walt Whitman or, if you prefer, the soulful ground Walt Whitman has become, shone invisible green in the real grass at Pisa. There was an embrace. There was a conversation of silences between one (Ezra) and one (Walt). I really believe this. And the conversation left a trace: the phosphorescence of "Canto LXXXI." Read it again. The rapture is still aglow, friendly and ready to hand.

Works Cited

The Bhagavad Gita, trans. Juan Mascaro. London: Penguin Books Ltd., 1962.

Ezra Pound. *The Cantos of Ezra Pound*. New York: New Directions, 1970.

Thomas Traherne. *Poems, Centuries, and Three Thanksgivings*. Oxford: Oxford University Press, 1966.

Henry David Thoreau. *Journal, Volume 1: 1837-1844*, eds. Elizabeth Hall Witherell et al. Princeton: Princeton University Press, 1981.

————. *Henry David Thoreau*, ed. Robert Sayre. New York: Literary Classics of the United States, 1985.

Walt Whitman. *Poetry and Prose.*, ed. Justin Kaplan. New York: Literary Classics of the United States, 1982.

IX

This is the ninth and last of these little essays. Time to rest now, and just enough time to show an ecstasy consistent with repose. I have a ready mind to turn to the Pastoral.

It is March 4th, Mardi Gras, 2003 and, Reader, you have a strange advantage of me. I am writing in the month whose name means war, whose name is taken from the god of the most ungodly practice humans use. You know the outcome or dear avoidance of events I merely dread and decry. Heaven help us either end of the Lent begins tomorrow. Today, I am writing in a cottage in Alabama, far from home. Outside my window across a cold yard of mud and brittle leaves, clumps of blackbirds come and go, contending with loose ranks of chubby robins. A godly strife. A good cacophony. And beneath them the ground that seems inert is, we know, already in throes of springtime ecstasy, soon to break out as Alabama grass and flowers. Cold pastoral, but never cold for long. My expectations rest at the window. The strife of the birds and its sharp sounds are an instance of repose to me, a moment whose inclination is towards an ecstasy, sure as sure can be. I think of John Cage: "I have nothing to say, and I am saying it." Too, I think of a wonderful sentence form *The Dragons of Eden* in which Carl Sagan avowed:

But absence of evidence is not evidence of absence.

The earth beneath the birds is cold and still, no evidence of the springtime surely rising. And rise it does, right now, resting only at the surface a few days more. It is rest enough. There is still time, a still time, while time is never still. I have a ready mind for the Pastoral.

The poems of Andrew Marvell have always resounded to me as miracles of calm expressed ecstatically. They profuse the pastoral moment through quiet frenzies which, even at their most methodical, remain wild. Models of rest in action, they show the one repose I am most eager to believe. Remember "The Garden"

What wondrous life is this I lead!
Ripe apples drop about my head;
The luscious clusters of the vine
Upon my mouth do crush their wine;
The nectarine, and curious peach,
Into my hands themselves do reach;
Stumbling on melons, as I pass,
Ensnared with flowers, I fall on grass.

The exclamation breaks forth from effortlessness. And the ravishing surround, far beyond mere providence and freedom, is a wilding. Here is the Fall, as they say, repairs the Fall, a further Adam enthroned on grass. This garden grows bacchantes and, in its ecstasy, makes a god of the downed man resting. And what is the name of the god? What is the particular virtue of his lavish repose? William Empson, in *Some Versions of Pastoral*, says it plain:

> Happiness, again, names a conscious state, and yet involves the idea of things falling right, happening so, not being ordered by an anxiety of the conscious reason. (125)

In the pastoral moment, rest is sovereign, and happiness is both the source *and* substance of its reign. In "The Garden," Marvell finds a wonder-working power, something which, in our own time, Denise Levertov called "the deep intelligence" of peace. From the depths of an effulgent rest, original wisdom shines.

Meanwhile the mind, from pleasures less,
Withdraws into its happiness:
The mind, that ocean where each kind
Does straight it own resemblance find,
Yet it creates, transcending these,
Far other worlds, and other seas,
Annihilating all that's made
To a green thought in a green shade.

"Original" is the meaning of green, and in the annihilation of labor ("all that's made"), original green gives shade and shelter to the godly man.

As Empson puts it, "the calm of Nature gives the poet an immediate self-knowledge" (126), i.e. a wisdom unmediated even by poetry itself. Earth's ecstasy is God's effortless knowledge of God. And it is also *our* selves and *our* peace resting in that knowledge. Transcendence does not quit the garden. It arrives and arrives, green after green, at further repose.

Rest is the place where innocence does its best work. From earliest utterance, Pastoral has espoused (and, in itself, sometimes embodied) idyllic production of real repose. To paraphrase Blake, effort is in love with the productions of rest. Pastoral simply unstops the music of that love. Like Marvell's mower in "The Mower against Gardens," it turns away from the harsh enforcement of effort (one of which is human society, I know, and another of which is war, as in "war effort" – Pastoral also suggests the perhaps disturbing possibility that true peace is ultimately sociopathic – as Jean-Jacques Rousseau opined, one can be a citizen or a man, but never both – shepherds sing one at a time, never together), and in turning, Pastoral discovers the will of Nature freely expressed and innocence running wild.

> Where willing nature does to all dispense
>   A wild and fragrant innocence:
> And fauns and fairies do the meadows till,
>   More by their presence than their skill.

Here is the equal distribution of wildness, dispensed like a fragrance, freely and without work. This is peace: the displacement of skill by presence. Peace is the sovereignty of presence. Allen asked us "When can I go to the supermarket and buy what I need with my good looks?" ("America"). Only the Pastoral can answer, and only the Pastoral's further Adams, enthroned on grass, can take such answering to heart. Damn near deified in the moments of rest, these marvelous Adams may see with divine eyes what divinity sees: the peace that passeth all the efforts of understanding. Thoreau (surprise!), my best-beloved sociopathic swain, showed such a moment to the best advantage I know in *Walden*, early on, at the very end of "Where I Lived, and What I Lived For."

Time is but the stream I go a-fishing in. I drink at it; but while I drink I see the sandy bottom and detect how shallow it is. Its thin current slides away, but eternity remains. I would drink deeper; fish in the sky, whose bottom is pebbly with stars. I cannot count one. I know not the first letter of the alphabet. I have always been regretting that I was not as wise as the day I was born.

(92-93)

Confluent with eternity, time shows a sky teeming with fish, and stars strewn across streambeds. No writing can capture them. No 'rithmetic can count them. Only effortlessness, momentarily consistent with divinity, can begin to share their peace.

Yet there is nothing more important to believe and to propound (if only to ourselves alone) than the forward, active increase peace projects from one eternal moment to the next. Marvell's idylls are not dioramas. The cabin at Walden Pond was no retreat, but rather a staging ground for peaceful excursions. The greening of thought and shade is an open system. A stream, however strewn with stars, still flows. In one of his earliest poems, "The K," Charles Olson, proposing his own mortality, finds an opening through which Pastoral works a way.

> I shall not see the year 2000
> unless I stem straight from my father's mother,
> break the fatal male small span.
> If that is what the tarot pack proposed
> I shall hang out some second story window
> and sing, as she, one unheard liturgy
>
> Assume I shall not.
> Is it of such concern when what shall be
> already is within the moonward sea?
>
> Full circle: an end to romans, hippocrats, and christians.
> There! Is a tide in the affairs of men to discern

Shallows and miseries shadows from the cross,
ecco men and dull copernican sun.
Our attention is simpler
The salts and minerals of the earth return
The night has a love for throwing its shadows around a man
a bridge, a horse, the gun, a grave.

Here, speculation wakes from its odic dream. (Note the near rhyme of "unheard liturgy" with Keats' unheard melodies whose cold pastoral could not find a way.) Full circle is not a closed circle. Time is concerned with eternity, and resting from the idle fear of death ("Is it of such concern…?") Olson wakes to a new repose borne forward by "the moonward sea." Empson describes such waking as

> …knowing that you know that you know, reconciling the remaining unconscious with the increasing consciousness, uniting in various degrees perception and creation, the one and the many..
>
> (145)

Rest is increase, trust, and new creation. Olson wakes to exclaim – "There!" – and what the exclamation adds is Pastoral discernment. Waking from labor to a full repose, he sees the work of fulfillment always and already underway. Olson's eye ("Our attention is simpler") confirms the truth of what his master, Whitehead, once avowed: "actual fact includes in its own constitution real potentiality which is referent beyond itself" (*Process and Reality* 112-113). Every opened eye is the resurrection and the life. Pastoral rests upon this and sets to work. I think of another poet, at the very end of his writing life this time. In Ronald Johnson's posthumous sequence, *The Shrubberies*, I find a one-line poem which offers inexhaustible repose.

> Yes Heaven/being/garden

The particular Heaven is already, by virtue of being, beyond itself: i.e. a garden. One Pastoral is already many. Rest easy. Eden's ahead. "There!" Peace works. It's a Pastoral discernment.

Outside my window this morning, first Sunday in Lent 2003, a cat as sleek and blacker than the blackbirds hunts across the mud and brittle leaves. He stops suddenly, remaining motionless a long time looking up into a tree. It's easy to follow his eyes and easy also then to share his particular rapture. There in the branches, also motionless, also fixed in attention, is a gray-brown squirrel with a tail so long and so absolutely pure pure white it's wonderful. No sleep could rest my eyes so well as does the blackness of the cat or the whiteness of that squirrel's tail. Each is a particular heaven, and in myself I feel a resurrection weeks ahead of time.

Pastoral discernment entrusts repose to the eye where vision rests in peace, in power. I come now to the end of these little essays, at the beginning of Lent and on the brink, it seems, of a new war. Reader, you may already contend with unimaginable outcomes. Good or ill, of course you do. For myself, I'll keep a ready mind for the Pastoral. Its power rests in a black cat's rapture and in a squirrel's unaccountable purest white. I think of the final stanzas of Ezra's "Canto XLIX."

> Sun up; work
> sundown; to rest
> dig well and drink of the water
> dig field; eat of the grain
> Imperial power is? and to us what is it?
>
> The fourth; the dimension of stillness.
> And the power over wild beasts.

The sun's full circle is never closed. The day is an open system. The work of peace is self-sustaining. "Imperial power is? and to us what is it?" A laborious hallucination. I have a mind for the Pastoral because I have seen with my own eyes the power of stillness when stillness is given time.

Works Cited

William Empson. *Some Versions of Pastoral*. New York: New Directions, 1974.

Allen Ginsberg. *Howl*. San Francisco: City Lights Books, 1956.

Ronald Johnson. *To Do as Adam Did*. Jersey City: Talisman House, 2000.

Andrew Marvell. *The Complete Poems*. New York: Penguin Books, 1972.

Charles Olson. *Selected Writings*. New York: New Directions, 1966.

Ezra Pound. *The Cantos of Ezra Pound*. New York: New Directions, 1970.

The Bittern's Eye

Joyful Noise:
The Gospel Sound
of Henry D. Thoreau

Now at Sundown I hear the hooting of an owl – hoohoo hoo
– hoorer – hoo…I rejoice that there are owls. They represent
the stark twilight unsatisfied thoughts I have.
　　—*Journals*, November 18, 1851

Some chickadees come flitting close to me, and one utters its
spring note, *phe-be*, for which I feel under obligations to him.
　　—*Journals*, January 9, 1858

I hear in several places the low dumping notes of awakened
bullfrogs, what I call their pebbly notes, as if they were cracking
pebbles in their mouths; not the plump *dont dont* or *ke dont*,
but *kerdle dont dont.*
　　—*Journals*, May 10, 1858

When, in doleful dumps, breaking the awful stillness of our
wooden sidewalk on a Sunday, or, perchance, a watcher in the
house of mourning, I hear a cockerel crow far or near, I think to
myself, "There is one of us well, at any rate," and with a sudden
gush return to my senses.
　　—"Walking"

The poems of a day begin presently with sound, and they
continue so. Henry David Thoreau, devoted friend of the
days, wrote continually, and still the writing makes the
sound of poems. Devotion is competent to every art. It pays perfect
attention, and in the economy of poetry (anything written attentively
is a poem, whatever else befalls), attention offers a presence to all
sounds and to what becomes of sound in words. In his *Journals* and in
books and essays collected out of them, Thoreau imagines unmediated

becoming, effortlessly. Sound becomes sense without even trying. An owl hoots and Thoreau rejoices in the instantaneous and unintended representation of his thought. A chickadee "utters its spring note," and Thoreau is under easy obligations he repays in kind: "*phe-be*," faithfully inscribed. Nothing is lost or stolen in translation because nothing is translated. Shaped by senses actually present, onomatopoeia makes sense. And when I read, it makes a sense in me. I am awakened with the bullfrogs by a noise Thoreau has somehow made my own. If I have a noise in mind, I must be somewhere, hearing it. And Thoreau is there beside me, untranslating all the while. I write poems because I love the sound of poems. My faith rests there. And Thoreau assures me faith is not misplaced. Every line, even before it is a line, and ever afterwards if it is true, instances the onomatopoeic sense of being somewhere in particular at a particular point in time. In poetry, the particular is good health to me, and saneness. As Thoreau explains, sound returns us to our sense. From doleful spells of inwardness, we are startled awake. The day is well, and it says so.

> But the music is not in the tune; it is in the sound.
> (*Journals*, June, 25, 1852)

Unscored, unscripted, the sense of the day is the day itself. It makes no references. Its forms transpire, indistinguishable by me from evidence of my senses. Where I put my faith I put myself. I find myself there, in passing, and there my feelings transpire, indistinguishable from the day. Thoreau's devotion to the hale sense of all sounds sets his words in the presence of presences: each is particular, not separate; each is musical, but not recognizable in the easy way of tunes. Always original, a sound declares itself unprecedented. And of course, of course that is what I believe about true feeling. *This has never happened to me before.* Reading a poem I hear a sound unheard until now. Making a poem, I utter sounds whose sense is sudden and particular to the hour. In *Walden*, Thoreau realized that even an echo is "an original sound" and "not merely a repetition," and it elapses over circumstances of space and time (treetops and sunrises) particular to itself. In tuneless restless sound Thoreau discovers a keener presence of mind. He abandons his faculties to his senses. Poetry, like freedom, like love, should always be unrecognizable, particularly to itself. It abandons poetry to become a poem. In reckless devotion, Thoreau becomes the stranger who is effortless to know.

Where there is sense, experience arrives. And so does death. In the intervals, effort serves the more to postpone experience – change of circumstances, change of world – than to pronounce it. So often, work is the delay of weal and woe. Early in the history of our Republic, Thoreau upends the work ethic, averring it a distraction from the urgent business of the day: life and death. Habits of effort, ritual and piecemeal, muffle extraordinary sounds of transformation. In a wonderful biography, *The Days of Henry Thoreau*, Walter Harding offers a glimpse of the man in undistracted extremity. The occasion is the death of Helen Thoreau, his elder sister.

> Helen died on June 14, 1849, aged only thirty-six. The funeral was held in the home on the eighteenth with both the Unitarian and the Trinitarian ministers in attendance. Thoreau sat seemingly unmoved with his family through the service, but as the pallbearers prepared to remove the bier, he arose and, taking a music box from the table, wound it and set it to playing a melody in a minor key that seemed to the listeners "like no earthly tune." All sat quietly until the music was over.

A moment of true feeling interrupts the inertial motion of ritual. Grief defies a senseless consolation, and the defiance is a sound, "a melody like no earthly tune." Helen, departed from Earth, is sounded no sound of Earth by her attentive brother. The onomatopoeia of extinction is a mechanical minor key. The sound of grief, whose object only is unearthly, employs no words. To speak of death, say nothing.

And Thoreau remained sound upon the efforts of speech, even to the end. Harding relays this telling vignette of a visit from one Parker Pillsbury to Thoreau only a few days before the writer's death.

> "Then I spoke only once more to him, and cannot remember my exact words. But I think my question was substantially this: 'You seem so near the brink of the dark river, that I almost wonder how the opposite shore may appear to you.' Then he answered, 'One world at a time.'"

Effortlessly, all sounds here. Elsewhere is a work of fiction worrying the minor keys.

> A child loves to strike on a tin pan or other ringing vessel
> with a stick, because, its ears being fresh, sound, attentive, and
> percipient, it detects the finest music in the sound, at which all
> nature assists. Is not the very cope of the heavens the sounding
> board of the infant drummer? So clear and unprejudiced ears
> hear the sweetest and most soul-stirring melody in tinkling
> cowbells and the like (dogs baying the moon), not to be
> referred to association, but intrinsic in the sound itself; those
> cheap and simple sounds which men despise because their ears
> are dull and debauched. Ah, that I were so much a child that
> I could unfailingly draw music from a quart pot! Its little ears
> tingle with the melody. To it there is music in sound alone.
>   (*Journals*, June 9, 1852)

Music – sustained, passionate, tenacious – remains innocent of effort. It is a feeling that persists in the act of hands, breath and senses. As melody, persistence makes the action of sound easy and sweet. Every day, Thoreau went out of the house of mourning to meet his senses where the music never stopped. Undebauched, undulled, never so much begun as continuing, the music of the day is ever available: "cheap and simple." From the available music, Thoreau could easily draw a full day's measure of poetry and truth, as above, in the innocent insistence of "sound alone." Our senses make tenacity a mere matter of waking (and of walking) to the world. There, uninterrupted by insensible referral, we find everything to be intrinsic. We find no duplication. Every sound originates with itself. And so, as a passage from *A Week on the Concord and Merrimack Rivers* believes, "The heart is forever inexperienced." Presence is percussion. All being makes a sound and another and then another. The truth and poetry of being are ever present unprepared, all parts particular. Here in the world, hearts hear, and a new heart beats in every sound.

Far in the night, as we were falling asleep on the bank of the Merrimack, we heard some tyro beating a drum incessantly, in preparation for a country muster, as we learned, and we thought of the line, --

"When the drum beat at the dead of night."

We could have assured him that his beat would be answered, and the forces be mustered. Fear not, thou drummer of the night; we too will be there. And still he drummed on in the silence and the dark. This stray sound from a far-off sphere came to our ears from time to time, far, sweet, and significant, and we listened with such an unprejudiced sense as if for the first time we heard at all. No doubt he was an insignificant drummer enough, but his music afforded us a prime and leisure hour, and we felt that we were in season wholly. These simple sounds related us to the stars. Ay, there was a logic in them so convincing that the combined sense of mankind could never make me doubt their conclusions. I stop my habitual thinking, as if the plow had suddenly run deeper in its furrow through the crust of the world. How can I go on, who have just stepped over such a bottomless skylight in the bog of my life? Suddenly old Time winked at me, -- Ah, you know me, you rogue, -- and news had come that IT was well. That ancient universe is in such capital health, I think undoubtedly it will never die. Heal yourselves, doctors; by God I live.
(from "Monday," *A Week on the
Concord and Merrimack Rivers*)

It really works. A present attention to particular sound realizes a place relating a place of one's own therein: a new world and new words; a poem. Hearing the real, incessant drum-taps straying through the dark, Thoreau is instantly "in season wholly," i.e., alert and fertile, i.e., present for a change. And change comes. The logic of the onomatopoeic instant overturns all convictions and previous logic. It is a wilding of habit. It is a deeper ground. It is a poem, as only poetry could overstep a skylight in a bog. The wink of Time in allegorical rough-and-ready assures us that Time is well. Surely the well-being of Time is news that stays news: i.e., a poem.

> It is not words that I wish to hear or to utter – but relations that I seek to stand in…
> (*Journals*, December 22, 1851)

Sounds occur to our hearing: *to* our hearing. They are immediately related, and we receive them in unique relationship. From Thoreau, I learn that poetry is not words primarily. Not even words are words originally. First comes sound. Standing or walking in his faith, Thoreau was always positioned to hear what Whitman, in a place, called "the origin of all poems." Poetry is a first relation to the sounds of a day and only subsequently the relating of itself in sentences and lines. And what comes first is, eventually, enough. Composer Charles Ives, the most articulate Thoreauvian of all, once announced "American music is already written." In the moments of days, for anyone standing in good relation to the sounds, American poetry is also already written. Thoreau says so.

> Above all, we cannot afford not to live in the present. He is blessed over all mortals who loses no moment of the passing life in remembering the past. Unless our philosophy hears the cock crow in every barnyard within our horizon, it is belated. That sound commonly reminds us that we are growing rusty and antique in our employments and habits of thought. His philosophy comes down to a more recent time than ours. There is something suggested by it that is a newer testament – the gospel according to this moment.
> ("Walking")

By the sound of things, unbelated is eternal. I awaken to no immediate danger. The gospel is right on time.

They Drank an Arrowhead:
Henry Thoreau &
Ronald Johnson

What loving astronomer has ever fathomed the ethereal depths
of the eye?
(Henry Thoreau, "Love" 324)

I have come to believe that Ronald Johnson was Henry Thoreau's
speculated astronomer, the poet whose optical allusions fathomed
facts first brought to light by light itself. And I find, as ever, that belief
makes reading more than possible; belief makes reading true. The eyes
of Thoreau freed his faith from creeds and custom. Johnson, thrilled by
the view, found a keen Way through Thoreau and saw the Way actually
strewn. Twinned visionaries now to my mind, they amplify Love's
answering question wildly, as in George Herbert's formula: Who made
the eyes but I?" ("Love III").

I've been aware of Ronald Johnson's poetry for only a few years.
One of very many, I'm sure, I first read it on the recommendation of
Guy Davenport's *The Geography of the Imagination*. The great scholar
had only to note "Mr. Johnson's transcendentalism" and that "he
came by it honestly" (194) to send me out looking for *Ark*. I opened
and read at haphazard, right away alighting on "Ark 74, Arches VIII
(from Thoreau's Journals)." There, I found express affiliation with my
favorite of all American texts, and then more than affiliation: a deep
understanding and rhyming practice. Johnson had found ideal passages
to pass the practice of Henry Thoreau forward, and he had forwarded
them in perfect time.

> "I look under the lids of time,
>   left without asylum
> to gather a new measure

through aisles of ages
   art, every stroke of the chisel
     enter own flesh and bone

without moving a finger
   turning my very brain
     reflected from the grass blades"

Here was a poet who, with Thoreau, gladly professed measures and newness to be "gathered," not made, a poet whose authorship explicitly depends from the authority of facts found as they are. In *The Line's Eye*, Elisa New has written that "the Concord gardener" learned "to let ripeness guide the picking" (111). "Ark 74" makes clear that Ronald Johnson learned the same. In poetry, learning is meaning, and Johnson was not ashamed to find it, in the deepest senses (as eyes go deeply to the brain), effortless. "Ark 74" was gladly made "without moving a finger." Gladness is key because, as Charles Olson somewhere said, "efforts are efforts." The sauntering *Journals* of Thoreau, as well as all the books made from them, propose a heroic unoriginality. The garden is always already there when the gardener arrives. Ask Adam. (Trebly apt is the fact that Johnson's *Selected Poems* is subtitled *To Do as Adam Did* from the fist line of *Ark's* "Beam 30," which is itself taken from Traherne's "The Apostasy." Traherne is the single greatest precursor of Thoreau, although the Concord gardener could not possibly ever have read him.) As Elisa New has shown, when we read Thoreau, we "watch a self's consolidation of itself in nature reversed by nature's weedy, friendly occupation of that self" (111). In "Ark 74," Ronald Johnson is likewise occupied by Henry Thoreau. And the fact is more than friendly. Because of Time's fact, it is a furthering.

And so I began to read his *Ark* straight through, finding the spirit and efflorescence of Thoreau bright from the outset. The practice of the poetry of fact, of what "Beam 2" celebrates as "Exactitude," makes common cause and conscience between the two writers. The surveyor's art which led Thoreau to see a line as Seen, as Found, continues in leading through *Ark's* early moves: the dancing, specific, blissfully located behaviors of atoms and the eye. Measure is a site. Sighted as seen, as given, it makes new myth.

I would so state facts that they shall be significant shall be myths or mythologic.
(Thoreau, *A Year in Thoreau's Journal: 1851*, 284)

The human eye, a sphere of waters and tissue, absorbs an energy that has come ninety-three million miles from another sphere, the sun. The eye may be said to be sun in other form.
(Johnson, "Beam 4")

Thoreau and Johnson can offer their mythologies as practical, entirely credible matters because they (and we) have seen them made. And thus they share a singular compulsion to come, literally to *come* to their senses.

> Linkings, inklings
> around the stem & branches of the nervetree –
> shudder and shutterings, sensings.

> SENSE *sings.*
> "A world where chaos and cosmos are interlaced and superimposed,
> where anything may happen,
>
> but nothing happens twice"
>
> --perceive! Perceive! Reality is "make" believe.
> (Johnson, "Beam 8")

Whatever things I perceive with my entire man – those let me record – and it will be poetry.
(Thoreau, *A Year* 188)

No method nor discipline can supersede the necessity of being forever on the alert. What is a course of history, or philosophy, or poetry, no matter how well selected, or the best society, or the most admirable routine of life, compared with the discipline

of looking always at what is to be seen? Will you be a reader, a
student merely, *or a seer? Read your fate, see what is before you,
and walk on into futurity.* (Thoreau, *Walden* 411)

Sense is revelation. The future is apparent to every opened eye.
Thoreau and Johnson were heliotropic Puritans. Jonathan Edwards
could joy to avow "Absolute sovereignty is what I love to ascribe to
God" ("Personal Narrative" 313). As I continued into *Ark,* I more and
more heard the avowal implicit in every written word of Thoreau's: i.e.
the absolute sovereignty of light. Thoreau and Johnson wrote what
they wrote in the sure and certain sense of a continuous radiance.

Eden, glossolalia of light
Mountain the gods stept from, spoke to fork
some sparkling *logos*
as *O hoher Baum im Orh!*
quadricornutus serpens, caduceus phantastikon, or
la ou nos la voions plus espesse
vas, at the same time orb and eggshaped
O
Matrix of Harmonies
Orders, opening back, beyond, and within, Laocoön of cocoon
Splint crystal, *glaux,* grey matter spun
'Out of thy head I sprung'
thread not a dream by a single Being, but one of *omni-*
silk-seed of waves hummed back
vast cortex
tensile, unstill

He who "world chair fire,
and have the wind move in regiments
of cubed air"
(As Bohm posited: at zeropoint
of energy
a cubic centimeter of space = 10,000,000,000 tons

uranium) underneathunder

unutterable number

an intricate quiet
centripetal

FIAT

he who
obsessed by light
possessed by sight:

cellophane in cellophane of salamander slid within a flame
(Johnson, "Beam 14")

There is more day to dawn. The sun is but a morning star.
(Thoreau, *Walden* 587)

And then I came to read "Beam 15," a passage from Thoreau's
journal entry dated August 17, 1851. The passage is accompanied by no
comment. Neither does Johnson offer any "variations on a theme" or
lyrical update. He simply and gigantically gives the passage the title
of "Cornerstone." Beyond doubt, to learn what was a-building in this
Ark, I would want to study this passage most, most closely. And to my
surprised happiness, I already had. It comes from one of the longest
and most beautiful entries in all the thousands of pages of the *Journals.*
As such, it is a cornerstone to Thoreau and to Thoreau-studies. Read
from start to finish (and I urge you to read it so), it entertains literally
every mood and natural piety of Thoreau's art, beginning in the
morning and ending with a goldfinch. And the passage excerpted by
Johnson is its mysterious physical heart, a passage which, only a few
weeks before I'd begun reading *Ark,* had moved me to write a poem of
my own, "Hypethral" (*There Are Three* 42). As ripeness is indeed a very
good guide, I was guided and ready to read this "Beam 15."

Beam, 15 Cornerstone

Thoreau: "How can that depth be fathomed where a man may
see himself reflected? The rill I stopped to drink at I drink in

more than I expected. I satisfy and still provoke the thirst of thirsts. I do not drink in vain. I mark that brook as if I had swallowed a water snake that would live in my stomach. I have swallowed something worth the while. The day is not what it was before I stopped to drink. Ah, I shall hear from that draught! It is not in vain that I have drunk. I have drunk an arrowhead. It flows from where all fountains rise. How many ova have I swallowed? Who knows what will be hatched within me? There were some seeds of thought, methinks, floating in that water, which are expanding in me. The man must not drink of the running streams, the living waters, who is not prepared to have all nature reborn in him — to suckle monsters. The snake in my stomach lifts his head to my mouth at the sound of running water. When was it that I swallowed a snake? I have got rid of the snake in my stomach. I drank of stagnant waters once. That accounts for it. I caught him by the throat and drew him out, and had a well day after all. Is there not such a thing as getting rid of the snake which you have swallowed with young, when thoughtless you stooped and drank at stagnant waters, which has worried you in your waking hours and in your sleep ever since, and appropriated the life that was yours? Will he not ascend into your mouth at the sound of running water? Then catch him boldly by the head and draw him out, though you may think his tail be curled about your vitals —

Finding my earlier inspiration here engrossed in *Ark*, I could only find more than I'd so far seen to believe. Here, Johnson lays his cornerstone on a radiant conjunction, a same anew, a draught redrafted but unfinished still. Placing it so, he invites us deeply to see the unoriginal fresh immensity of his purposes. And deep is close.

The passage concerns real myth, which is to say myth-making: not something customarily believed, but something enacted and seen to be done. Thoreau, and with Thoreau, Johnson, here describe practices prior to Religion, behaviors beyond Law. They were antinomians in the active, innocent sense. (Like Blake before, each propounded the vigor of unoriginal innocence, one whose unharming energies vivify, perhaps even maintain, the originating world-as-found.) In this spirit, Johnson later offers his right, opened handprint as the entirety of "Beam 18." In this spirit, only a few lines above the passage constituting this "Beam 15," Thoreau exclaims "Ah I would not tread on a cricket in whose song is such a revelation – so soothing and cheering to my ear. O keep my senses pure!" (*A Year* 158). And so we come to those draughts and purgations excerpted as *Ark's* "Cornerstone." The snake of "stagnant waters" is the monster of habit's depravity, the monster whose maculate priority (called culture, called society, called dogma, called law and, sometimes, I) befouls originary waters. And so the draught of an arrowhead and ova from the running stream becomes an improvised rite of aversion; our poets meant to cleanse their vessels from the inside out. Too, the rite is an antiquity renewed. Thoreau was as keen on the practice of the same anew as was Johnson. We have seen this snake before, in the *Oresteia* of Aeschylus. It is the snake of Clytemnestra's dream.

> *Orestes*
> Do you know the dream, too? Can you tell it to me right?
>
> *Chorus*
> She told me herself. She dreamed she gave birth to a snake.
>
> *Orestes*
> What is the end of the story then? What is the point?
>
> *Chorus*
> She laid it swathed for sleep as if it were a child.
>
> *Orestes*
> A little monster. Did it want some kind of food?
>
> *Chorus*
> She herself, in the dream, gave it her breast to suck.
>
> *Orestes*
> How was her nipple not torn by such a beastly thing?
>
> *Chorus*
> It was. The creature drew in blood along with the milk.

Orestes
No void dream this. It is the vision of a man.
(*The Libation Bearers*, trans. Lattimore, 112)

And it is the snake which, proliferated into the serpent chorus of Eumenides, the "goddesses beneath the ground" (*The Eumenides* 138), vents "the deadly anger of the mother snake (139) upon Orestes in his quest for cleanness and innocence renewed. Thoreau honored Aeschylus and had translated him seriously as early as 1839. In a journal entry from that year, he praised the dramatic poet in words which, to me, perfectly describe the accomplishment of *Ark* as I have learned to read it from the "Cornerstone" of "Beam 15."

Let the seer bring down his broad eye to the most stale and trivial fact, and he will make you believe it a new planet in the sky.
(*Selected Journals* 42)

Thoreau and Johnson compound the future of antiquity by refreshing and broadening the eye. Ceded its just originality, a fact is a cosmos. The Eumenides of self and of all custom have no power over it. Thus the cosmographer's genius is unoriginal unto everlasting, mapping without maps and with eyes wide open. Thus did surveyor Thoreau discover dawns without end in *Walden*. Thus did the exacting wild-eyed Ronald Johnson find fountains leaping in each beam and spire and arch of his *Ark*. He drank an arrowhead, and it leaps up in the very last lines of his book:

Origins great aorta
leaved from the wrist up, but
yet to attain the skies

all arrowed a rainbow midair,
ad astra per aspera
countdown for Lift Off
("Ark 99, Arches XXXIII")

Works Cited

Aeschylus. *Oresteia*, trans. By Richmond Lattimore. Chicago: University of Chicago Press, 1953.

Guy Davenpoert. *The Geography of the Imagination*. Berkeley: North Point Press, 1981.

Jonathan Edwards. "Personal Narrative," Collected in *Early American Writing*, ed. Giles Gunn. New York: Penguin Books, 1994.

George Herbert. "Love III," in *George Herbert and Henry Vaughan*. Oxford: Oxford University Press, 1986.

Ronald Johnson. *Ark*. Albuquerque, New Mexico: Living Batch Press, 1996.

———. *To Do as Adam Did*. Jersey City, New Jersey: Talisman House, 2000.

Elisa New. *The Line's Eye*. Cambridge, Massachusetts: Harvard University Press, 1998.

Donald Revell. *There Are Three*. Middletown, Connecticut: Wesleyan University Press, 1998.

Henry David Thoreau. *Selected Journals*, ed. Carl Bode. New York: The New American Library, 1967.

———. *A Year in Thoreau's Journal: 1851*, ed. Daniel Peck. New York: Penguin Books, 1993.

———. *Walden, Henry David Thoreau*, ed. Robert F. Sayre. New York: The Library of America, 1985.

———. "Love," in *Collected Essays and Poems*, ed Elizabeth Hall Witherell. New York: The Library of America, 2001.

Thomas Traherne. *Poems, Centuries and Three Thanksgivings*, ed. Anne Ridler. Oxford: Oxford University Press, 1966.

Pierre Reverdy: Poems Left Ajar

I love Reverdy for saying yes, though I don't believe it.
(Frank O'Hara, "Adieu to Norman,
Bonjour to Joan and Jean-Paul")

I am looking Gisele Freund's photo-portrait of Pierre Reverdy: a telling image or, rather, a complex of images tallying the mysteries of a plain man. The poet gazes from a bowed head, and so his eyes seem simultaneously lowered *and* raised. Behind him, tangled trees turn away from one another, partly escaping an implacable embrace. And beside him, a white wrought-iron chair tilts its seat at an impossible angle, escaping use. All is paused in perfect contrariness. Pierre Reverdy holds his fingers to his lips. He is deciding between silence and speech. It looks to me as though he will choose them both.

The poems of Reverdy articulate his portrait with bewildering clarity. As the great escape act of twentieth-century writing, they meticulously detail contradictions into which their motives and their maker disappear. Reverdy was an author of prolific reticence whose published novels, notebooks and volumes of poetry (there are more than a dozen of those) mount an enormous drama from which he turns aside, almost a little sadly, as though he could not find a place for himself in his own words. And so the anguish of the drama, never quite personal, becomes universal. Reverdy's substance and style wholly express his situation . Early and lastingly defined as *the* poet of Cubism, he nevertheless averred, "La poesie cubiste? Terme ridicule!" Spending the greater part of his adult life (from 1926 until his death in 1960) in and around the religious community of Solesmes, he drew main force for writing from his loss of faith, a loss he dated from 1928 onwards. A virtual recluse, he celebrated the splendor of friendship unstintingly: "Without my marvelous friendships, without Picasso, Braque, Gris, Apollinaire, I would have amounted to nothing." A transcendentalist poet of pure, sharp surfaces, Reverdy departs from us in every word's arrival. It is not surprising, then, that his great American translator and advocate, Kenneth Rexroth, should find in him both a simplicity inspiring to younger poets like Gary Snyder and Robert Creeley, as well as a "complex and secret logic" pointing, surely, towards the syntax and countrysides of their very different contemporary, John Ashbery. Regarded closely, the poems of Pierre Reverdy confirm even as they multiply the contradictions of their quiet fame. Indeed, it would be hard to find a better motto for them anywhere than in these closing, gnomic, utterly transparent lines of Ashbery's "These Lacustrine Cities":

> Tender and insouciant by turns, you see
> You have built a mountain of something,
> Thoughtfully pouring all your energy into this
>   single monument,
> Whose wind is desire starching a petal,
> Whose disappointment broke into a rainbow of tears.

For Reverdy, surfaces transcend their disappointed limits on just a touch. In "Central Heating," the touch is "a little light," and the light proliferates planes and imagery of the surface unto tender points of love.

> A little light
> Look a little light descends on your belly and
>   lights you up
> -- A woman stretches herself like a rocket--
> Over there in the corner a shadow reads
> Her bare feet are too pretty
>   (translated from the French by Kenneth Rexroth, l. 1-5)

At such a point, mentor and friend Apollinaire's technique of "straying" – "errer" – protracts the love by getting lost.

> Short circuit in the heart
> Breakdown in the motor
> What magnet holds me up
> My eyes and love have lost their way
>   (l. 6-9)

Here, love is a sad success, an escape into the next moment to which the past appears so dearly. Perception dissolves with eyesight the fragile compositions of a heart. Past and present are infolded into something new, something like love, but a little too clear to keep mysteries alive.

> At bottom everything we see is artificial
> Even your mouth
> Yes I get hot where your hand touches me
> The door is open and I don't go in
> I see your face and I don't believe it
> You're pale
> One night we were sad and wept on our trunk
> Men laughed down there
> Children strolled around almost naked
> The water was clear
> Copper wire conducts the light
> The sun and your heart are made of the same material
> (1. 14-25)

In the manner of central heating, Cubism is modern and efficient… and mundane. It ends with facts: water, wire, material. Reverdy wishes to escape with a separate heart and sun. And we are left with a poem, one whose ultimate conflation, like Apollinaire's at the end of his perfect lyric, "Annie," – "La dame et moi suivons presque le même rite" – means more than it can say, and says so, and ends there, transcending.

As it happens, transcendence is an opportunity (or option) opened by supernumerous dramas of a surface world. Reverdy, multiplying simple prepositions, assembles diversions. At a climax, these flash and glow. In clamorous pathos, the poet escapes.

> From the triangle of the sidewalks of the square
> all the wires start, and the scythe of the rainbow,
> broken behind the clouds.
> In the center the one who waits, blushes,
> not knowing where to stand.
> Everyone is looking and in that same place
> the wall reveals its wound.

The hand that closes the shutter disappears, the head
cut by the ray doesn't fall – and there remains
that illusion which at the same moment
drew everyone's eyes toward the drama that was being
   enacted,
opposite the sunset, against the window.
       ("…Is Ajar," translated from
           the French by John Ashbery)

As Ezra Pound would approve, these phrases "juxtapose in
beauty." (Or as Reverdy himself wrote in the March 1918 edition of
his magazine *Nord-Sud*, "The image is a pure creation of the mind.
It cannot be born from a comparison but from a juxtaposition of
two more or less distant realities.") The prepositions accrue unto
themselves a magical agency, an illusion of spectacular simultaneities.
Yet what has happened, what *is* happening, we cannot say. Through
a door "ajar" in the poem's method, poetry goes. Ordinary grammar
makes mystery. Who can follow?

At the very least, and hopefully, we can see the poet following
poetry along the pathway of a preposition: "toward" ("vers"). In this
direction, a substantial mystery, "love without an object," refreshes faith
in the secret logic by which Reverdy overleaps his surface world.

I no longer want to go away toward those vast bowls of evening
To grip the icy hands of the nearest shadows
I can no longer put off this look of despair
Nor reach the great cities waiting for me out there
Yet it is toward those formless faces that I go
Toward those moving lines which still imprison me
Those lines in my eyes trace in the vagueness
Those dim landscapes those mysterious days
Under cover of gray weather when love passes by
A love without an object burning night and day
Which wears out the lamp of my chest so weary
Of restraining the sighs which die in their tower
Blue distance hot countries white sands
Shore where gold tosses where laziness takes root
Tepid wharf where the sailor falls asleep

Treacherous water which comes to flatter the hard rock
Under the greedy sun which is browsing on the foliage
Thought heavy with sleep blinking
Light memories like curls on a forehead
Nights of sleep without waking in a bed too deep
Efforts put off until tomorrow
Smile of the sky sliding in the hand
But above all homesickness for that solitude
O closed heart O heavy heart O deep heart
You will never get used to sorrow
("Love Again," translated from
the French by John Ashbery)

The hurried, minimal landscapes here – "tower" and "tepid wharf"
and "white sands" – are surreal as any by Chirico and account well
for Breton's assertion, in the first surrealist manifesto, of Reverdy's
preeminence among the poets of his generation. In "Love Again,"
transcendental surrealist flight is called to a sudden halt by simplest
emotion: "homesickness." Extravagance becomes plain. Elusiveness
puts down roots, and these roots tap into human universal anguish,
the "deep heart" of "sorrow." Clearly, for Reverdy juxtaposition
accomplishes a great deal more than magic tropes. It makes a way to
wholeness and entirety. It makes a welcome for the ordinary and for
the strange in one quick voice.

Spoken at points of waking or dying from strange familiarities of
transcendence, the poems of Reverdy suffer those primary disjunctions
which define and mystify the human heart. They suffer the line breaks.
They suffer in images superseded by escape and erasure. Broken
vision keeps their Visions pure. It is the purity, the nearly sacramental
insistence of Reverdy's bewilderment that gives his work an authority
without question...without even access to question. Discontinuities
disappear under order of instants. And each instant is a love.

The hardly open eyes
            The hand on the other shore
The sky
            And everything that happens there
The leaning door

A head sticks out
From the frame
And through the shutters
You can see out
The sun fills everything
But the trees are still green
                    The falling hour
                    It gets warmer
And the houses are smaller
The passersby go less quickly
And always look up
                    The lamp shines on us now
Looking far away
We could see the light
                    Coming
We were happy
                    That evening
At the house where somebody waits for us
            ("The Same Number," translated from
                the French by Kenneth Rexroth)

In the pause between "that evening" and "the other house," we feel
the poet's heartbroken method. Happiness is lost from the start, being
wholly a nostalgia for intervals: the wordlessness between words,
the full sunlight fallen between two images. Here, with unmatched
elegance and delicacy, Reverdy anticipates our contemporary fret for
the shortfalls of language. With wide authority and tact, he neither
grieves nor seeks to mend. He steps away.

He steps without hope, but never despairingly. Nostalgia for the
intervals is not backward or bereft. Living in featureless anticipation,
it rushes beyond recognition really to see. Objective desires hearken
forward unbetrayed. Pierre Reverdy comes, then, to be numbered
(enlarging Hugh Kenner's beautiful phrase) among our century's
"stoic comedians." In company with Camus and Keaton, Beckett and
Apollinaire, he finds calm shores of departure in oblivion, and stars in
the void.

We pass elegantly along the void
          and don't fall
But sometimes something in us makes everything
  tremble
And the world ceases
          Our eyes are tricked
You don't hear the same sound anymore
The same voice
Behind the universe itself you can see
          A dancing silhouette
The series of portraits recalls nothing
          Of those you never knew
These people who stare at you
          Shiny frames preserve them
In the midst of those immobile faces
The only one alive
          Seems the calmest
He leaves never to return
To the room where the walls begin to smile
Nothing anymore but night rising to leave
          A footstep echoing on the flagstone
It grows cold
Your eyes lift to the stars
          ("Galleries," l. 43-65, translated from
          `the French by Kenneth Rexroth)

To Reverdy, cold and calm are a climate of limitless permission: permission to abscond, to escape, to transcend. He awaits no Word. In the coincidence of cosmic indifference and ineffable passion, Reverdy finds his perfect contrariness. It is not a conundrum. It is a pitch darkness filled with lights.

Works Cited

Ashbery, John. *Rivers and Mountains*. New York: Holt, Rinehart and Winston, 1966.

O'Hara, Frank. *The Selected Poems of Frank O'Hara*. New York: Random House, 1974.

Reverdy, Pierre. *Nord-Sud, Self defence, et autres ecrits sur l'art et la poesie 1917-1926*. Paris: Flammarion, 1975.

———. *Selected Poems*. Ed. Timothy Bent. Winston-Salem, NC: Wake Forest University Press, 1991.

———. *Selected Poems*. Ed. Trans Kenneth Rexroth. New York: New Directions, 1969.

The Must of an Ever:
Merwin's Totem Animal

The energies of W.S. Merwin sustain oracular lamentations for a wildness so far and so cruelly forgotten as not even to be sensibly absent anymore. Merwins' finest poems, the ones which after just a single reading seem to accomplish genetic information, begin at the far side of tragedy, a site of origins abandoned, a void where primal forces cross and stray. From there, the poems arise into purpose and purposeful movement, not quite hopefully, but ever something more than resigned to the effort of words. One of these, "Words from a Totem Animal," imagines first a void of brokenness and then a site of purposes so wholly other, so harshly alien, as to agonize the Wild.

> Distance
> is where we were
> but empty of us and ahead of
> me lying out in the rushes thinking
> even the nights cannot come back to their hill
> any time
>
> I would rather the wind came from outside
> from mountains anywhere
> from the stars from other
> worlds even as
> cold as it is this
> ghost of mine passing
> through me
> (I. 1-13)

"Words from a Totem Animal" is Merwin's animistic "Dream of the Rood" in which wildness, broken from its movement and earth, speaks contrary to nature from the unnatural place of Icon. Language is a ghost of nature clamoring in symbols: in this case, an animal's imago hammered into wood. Speech is a wind with no outside, and Merwin's animal feels a memory of the outside now as death.

> I know your silence
> and the repetition
> like that of a word in the ear of death
> teaching
> itself
> itself
> that is the sound of my running
> the plea
> plea that it makes
> which you will never hear
> (14-23)

Silence runs free, a perpetual motion and delay of beginnings. Deprived of silence by human symbology (call it the "dialect of the tribe"), totem animal can only repeat the word "death" whose synonyms are "itself / itself." Becoming an oracle, Merwin's creature writhes in oracular futility.

Totem is another name for trap, and wildness cannot shed its agony until it sheds its names. This dilemma flashes within almost all of Merwin's' very best poems. (I think especially of "Fly" whose final line so keenly condemns the keeping and the keepers of creatures: "I who have always believed too much in words.") The rostrum of voice is also a gibbet, and vocalizing, elegizing the Wild, poetry cannot help but entrap it more deeply, tormenting it with tender names throughout a lengthy lamentation. Poems are false hopes.

> I might have been right
> not who I am
> but all right
> among the walls among the reasons
> not even waiting
> not seen
> but now I am out in my feet
> and they on their way
> the old trees jump up again and again

strangers
there are no names for the rivers
for the days for the nights
I am who I am
oh lord cold as the thoughts of birds
and everyone can see me

Caught again and held again
again I am not a blessing
they bring me
names
that would fit anything
they bring them to me
they bring me hopes
all day I turn
making ropes
helping

My eyes are waiting for me
in the dusk
they are still closed
they have been waiting a long time
and I am feeling my way toward them

I am going up stream
taking to the water from time to time
my marks dry off the stones before morning
the dark surface
strokes the night
above its way
There are no stars
there is no grief
I will never arrive
I stumble when I remember how it was
with one foot
one foot still in a name

I can turn myself toward the other joys and their lights
but not find them
I can put my words into the mouths
of spirits
but they will not say them
I can run all night and win
and win

      (26-74)

What "might have been right," what might have retained the lordly
anonymity of "I am who I am," stumbles into dreams and into the
wishful thinking of captivity; "I can run all night and win / and win."
But tethered to a totem name, wildness still only writhes. Rhetoric
– "and win / and win" – is disembodiment itself writhing.

    Yet wildness is not finally resigned to wishing, nor do wishes fill
a void as full as actual sounds. Sound harrows the close confinement
of words and prayer. The whole body of Merwin's work avers that a
simple noise restores the strength of worlds. In the thrall of words, all
noises resound joyfully. Sound radiates. It is not a closed circuit of
significations. It opens. In the open, totem animal finds itself again
anew "as though I were almost there."

Dead leaves crushed grasses fallen limbs
the world is full of prayers
arrived at from
afterwards
a voice full of breaking
heard from afterwards
through all
the length of the night

I am never all of me
unto myself
and sometimes I go slowly
knowing that sound one sound
is following me from world

to world
and that I die each time
before it reaches me

When I stop I am alone
at night sometimes it is almost good
as though I were almost there
sometimes then I see there is
in a bush beside me the same question
why are you
on this way
I said I will ask the stars
Why are you falling and they answered
which of us

(75-100)

The bush *is* there. Its actual sound is a question and a way. Asked of the stars, the question is answered by numberless, nameless singularity: "which of us?" That is all the totem animal needs to hear. The passion of its actual renovation to new wildness begins.

Sound – pure sound – and the imminent interrogatives of being – bush and star – announce the advent of a new state. It is a wilder wildness revealed when imago is stripped bare and when questions are pared down to blessed silence.

I dreamed I had no nails
no hair
I had lost one of the senses
not sure which
the soles peeled from my feet and
drifted away
clouds
It's all one
feet
stay mine
hold the world lightly

Stars even you
have been used
but not you
silence
blessing
calling me when I am lost
(101-117)

The passion of totem animal is its release into invisible, speechless
unity: "It's all one." Merwin is our advocate of vital, even desperate
paradoxes: invisible (therefore Deep) imagism and the wordless poetic
sublime. His totem animal finds its help in these. Torn apart, it arises.
Silenced, it calls.

I have been waiting there
as a new
year finds the song of the nuthatch

Send me out into another life
lord because this one is growing faint
I do not think it goes all the way
(120-126)

Tender and calm in its recovered wildness, totem animal needs
no metaphysics. The void and its abandoned origins fade away to
incompleteness and representation: into words. The Wild is whole
and wholly new as "the song of the nuthatch," and equally uninscribed.
Poetry will not take us all the way. The Wild will.

Proper Rites

In poetry, evidence of mastery is first a sound and then a resonance; mastery is a consequence of the simple immediacy of words that bring forth truth. One of the gentlest men I ever knew, Elias Schwartz, a great teacher of prosody, introduced me to the sound and verity of John Skelton when he read this couplet aloud:

> It is generall
> To be mortall.

These remain my favorite lines of poetry. To me, they define mastery as a sound immediately and then continually true; they conduct a conviction to my mind and, I hope, to my behavior as a poet and man. The immediacy of imagination is in the movement of these lines. The physical qualities of the words somehow repair the mediating gaps in language between the material words and their meanings. This reparation ministers through sound, and the sound ministers through time. The whole of "Uppon a Deedmans Hed" moves by way of fleetingly close rhymes; but the sheer force of their velocity protracts these transitory propositions toward a future reader. The doctrine of only a moment—these lines go so quickly – instructs eternity. Mortality endures; the poem is a priest to its readers. It was William Carlos Williams who proposed that a "poet thinks with his poem." Skelton, thinking instantly aloud, thinks to me. *Myrres vous y* ("See yourself here"), he tells me, and so I do, and so he is my master. In the general mortality of his meaning, Skelton requires my own right and tender conduct.

In "Phyllyp Sparowe," Skelton requires the syllable itself to be right and tender. Lamenting the death of a sparrow, Skelton looses syllables of the Vespers of the Dead – "Pl ace bo" and "Di le si" – into pure sound and pitch – "Fa, re, my, my" – recalling the common sound of a sparrow's song. Onomatopoeia is the proper rite in this elegy over the soul of a sparrow. The proper poem evinces a passing sound. The sparrow is my master's master. He sings and dies. The lesson keens forward in every elegy, as every poem elegizes sound. *Myrres vous y* while breath remains.

In Robert Creeley's "Flowers," the simple presence of flowers can move our words into immediacy and a timely conviction. Delight and instruction happen to be one. There is no abstraction, no enduring misery or law, that can prevail over the particular immanence of flowers. The particular flower is a profusion of singularities, as Creeley so beautifully avows, apportioning his lines to one pure fact apiece. Each object is a whole thing unto itself; presence ends refraction. And the lesson of forgiveness shows itself in flowers, in the freedom of passing beauty.

Indeed, it has always been Creeley's *way* to discover comprehension and its techniques dissolving into the better air (or fragrance) of a Virtue or a Love. So in "Flowers," the taut, particular lines of the poetry ease into atonement. Craft disappears in peace. This way, this masterful trajectory, is wonderfully explained by a letter Creeley wrote to Charles Olson in 1951. He begins:

> A statement: there is no better poet than Hart Crane / August 15, 1951.

The plain bold proposal is the matter of its moment. Timeliness proceeds from faith. The letter goes on to enact a brilliantly detailed appreciation of seven of Hart Crane's lyric poems, emphasizing the sounds of vowels and consonantal shadings. Creeley thereby brings the poems into the present tense, into the proper rite of Presences.

> you are going to hear, if you can but listen, can but,
> in any sense, hear, sounds as incredible, as finely knit,
> caught, as any man ever wrote them

Creeley's point is to present and not to prove the sounds. And so he concludes his understanding with one exclamation:

> Dammit / isn't that gentle!

As in "Flowers," Creeley uses mastery to get beyond mastery, exemplifying craft as conduct. Forgiveness and gentleness design poetic motives. The lesson shows momentous virtue, and then it's done.

My poem "Arcady Siskiyou" was done early in the morning after an evening of jazz on a small town's fairground. The evening had been wonderful, with children and dancing and summer sounds mixing with the music. Driving home afterwards, we played the radio, and a ballad about a girl named Lily came on. Somehow, the several repetitions of "Lily" made onomatopoeic magic, bearing the earlier concert forward into the night, into sleep, and into my very first words upon waking. "Lily" had captured the virtue and duration of a sweet memory, and I wanted to make a poem saying so. I wanted my new-found faith in the sound "Lily" to resound with conviction. I thought of Skelton: of the moral force of his rhymes and of his sparrow's soulful song. Immediately I thought, too, of Creeley's couplet at the end of "Flowers." I'd felt an ecstatic gentleness in the music of the night before, and my two master poets, each in his own way and also as an ensemble, directed me towards entire faith in "Lily." "Lily" was the word to bring dear imagery and moments forward into the present and into immediate, perhaps eternal, keeping. I gave the poem over to "Lily," and, for me, it accomplished a sunrise to face the sinking moon of memory. The awkwardness of my Lily's insistent repetition felt eventually like grace. And grace is candor and the pleasure to say, really, my wife's kisses had been the deepest pleasures of the previous evening. "Arcady Siskiyou" ends there. This is the lesson, then, of mastery to me: candor and the awkward confidence of what is truth to tell.

John Skelton
Upon a Deedmans Hed

Skelton Laureat, upon a deedmans hed,
That was sent to hym from an honorable Jentyllwoman for
A token, Devysyd this gostly medytacyon in Englysh:
Convenable in sentence, Commendable, Lamentable,
Lacrymable,
Profitable for the soule.

Youre ugly tokyn
My mynd hath brokyn
From worldly lust;

For I have dyscust
We ar but dust,
And dy we must.
    It is generall
To be mortall:
I have well espyde
No man may hym hyde
From deth holow-eyed,
With synnews syderyd,
With bonys shyderyd,
With hys worme-etyn maw
And hys gastly jaw
Gaspyng asyde,
Nakyd of hyde,
Neyther flesh nor fell.
    Then by my councell,
Loke that ye spell
Well thys gospel:
For wherso we dwell,
Deth wyll us quell
And with us mell.
    For all oure pampered paunchys,
There may no fraunchys
Nor worldly blys
Redeme us from this:
Oure days be datyd
To be chekmatyd,
With drawttys of deth
Stopping oure breth;
Oure eyen synkyng,
Oure bodys stynkyng,
Oure gummys grynnyng,
Oure soulys brynnyng!
To whom then shall we sew
For to have rescew,
But to swete Jesu
On us then for to rew?
    O goodly chyld

Of Mary mylde,
Then be oure shylde!
That we be not exylyd
To the dyne dale
Of boteles bale,
Nor to the lake
Of fendys blake.
    But graunt us grace
To se thy face,
And to purchace
Thyne hevenly place
And thy palace,
Full of solace,
Above the sky,
That is so hy,
Eternally
To beholde and se
The Trynyte!
    Amen.

Excerpt from *Phyllyp Sparowe*

Pl ace bo,
       Who is there, who?
Di le xi,
       Dame Margery,
Fa, re, my, my
       Wherefore and why, why?
       For the sowle of Phyllyp Sparowe,
That was late slayn at Carowe,
Among the Nones Blake.
For that swete soules sake,
And for all sparowes soules
Set in our bede rolles,
Pater noster qui,
With an *Ave Mari,*
And with the corner of a Crede,
The more shal be your mede.

Whan I remember agayn
How mi Philyp was slayn,
Never halfe the payne
Was between you twayne,
Payramus and Thesbe,
As than befell to me:
I wept and I wayled,
The tearys downe hayled;
But nothynge it avayled
To call Phylyp agayne,
Whom Gyb our cat hath slayne.

      Gyb, I saye, our cat,
Worrowyd her on that
Which I loved best.
It can not be exprest
My sorowfull hevynesse,
But all without redresse;
For within that stounde,
Halfe slumbrynge, in a sounde
I fell downe to the grounde.

      Unneth I kest myne eyes
Towarde the cloudy skyes,
But when I dyd beholde
My sparrow dead and colde,
No creature but that wolde
Have rewed upon me,
To behold and se
What hevynesse dyd me pange:
Wherewith my handes I wrange
That my senaws cracked
As though I had ben racked,
So payned and so strayned
That no lyfe well ny remayned.

      I syghed and I sobbed,
For that I was robbed
Of my sparowes lyfe.
O mayden, wydow, and wyfe,
Of what estate ye be,

Of hye and lowe degre,
Great sorowe than ye myght se,
And lerne to wepe at me!
Such paynes dyd me frete
That myne hert dyd bete,
My vysage pale and dead,
Wanne, and blewe as lead:
The panges of hatefull death
Well nye had stopped my breath.

Robert Creeley
from *Flowers*

> *No knowledge rightly understood*
> *can deprive us of the mirth of flowers.*
> —Edward Dahlberg

No thing less than one thing
or more—

no sun
but sun—

. . . .

What truth is it
that makes men so miserable?

Days we die
are particular—

This life cannot be lived
Apart from what it must forgive.

Donald Revell
Arcady Siskiyou

Was circus once once Lily
Kisses once imagined are jazz bands

A black great musical man
In the heat of town
On the July fairground
Spread the flowers of his hands
We all for hours were imaginary babies
Lily the sound of water next morning
Lily the light across the sound
Sun a lily circus continuing
Faced the quarter moon down

So July
Like the skittering of dragonflies
Was kisses really

Purists Will Object

The poetry of John Ashbery is the most enabling that I know, an uninterrupted and beautifully various series of spurs and permissions. And it follows that I feel myself most enabled by my *un*certainties as to the specifics of his influence on how I think of poems and write them. His work surrounds more than it designates; it animates more than it names. That this is true of all the primary instigators of our avant gardes – Duchamp, Beckett, Cage, and others – encourages me to describe and avow the influence of Ashbery's poetry without at the same time feeling obliged to assign to it a fixed value or precise dynamic. My purpose in what follows is such an avowal through eight brief meditations on the enabling qualities of eight passages, each from a different Ashbery collection. Along the way, I hope not to define influences, but to witness the means by which influence happens. Definition would be a traduction. Influence is exemplary, after all, not metaphorical.

> But she, of course, was only an effigy
> Of indifference, a miracle
>
> Not meant for us, as the leaves are not
> Winter's because it is the end
> ("Illustration")

Influence begins as an incident of disturbance. It continues as a sequence of disturbances in a manner that Robert Lowell described as "stirring and blurring." The sequence proceeds unmethodically between the general and particular. This is how one begins to hear and be changed by Ashbery. The "she," the woman whom I would by habit imagine as any one of a number of idealities (erotic, aesthetic, organic or abstract) pre-empts my habitual response by being "only an effigy." Ashbery's poems often practice a pre-emptive lessness, an unexpected diminishment of figure and image which turns the canonical reflex into a pratfall and leaves the reader gazing bewilderedly up at what has been diminished. Reduced to an effigy, the "she" acquires an imaginative status and power that conventional exaltation could never have provided. By itself, this instance of inversion technique is enough to produce a *vertige*, a disturbance recognizably avant garde. But the momentum of the passage continues through several instances: the effigy, usually a product of satirical or outraged passions, is of "indifference," a caricature of no tone; and indifference, a state usually deprived of affect, is a "miracle," a liberating disturbance of natural law; and still the liberation is "not meant for us" although the double pause of a line and stanza break allows us plenty of leisure to imagine that it is and to begin to anticipate its precise form. Intention gains force though the denial of intention, just as Ashbery changes the way I understand poetic decorum by abjuring the accumulation of meaning that is decorum's conventional purpose. The phrases "mean" by failing to add up, by congregating possibilities, most of them contradictory, but not synthesizing them. The particular (e.g., the effigy) and the general (e.g., the undetailed miracle) no longer function as categories in such a congregation because Ashbery refuses to allow them to refer to anything beyond themselves. As winter is the literal, intentionless end of nature, this passage represents the literal, unaggressive end of metonymy. The feeling in the passage, simultaneously vivid and non-specific, exercises passion without imperiousness, reference without attitude. Where some readers find themselves resenting such indeterminacies as artless and unhelpful, I have, since first reading Ashbery as a student, in the little Carnegie-built library in Binghamton, New York, watching the pigeons homing at sunset to the green dome of the City Hall across the plaza from the window at which I read, felt exhilarated and companioned by such unimperiousness. The end of metonymy has meant for me the beginning of an unlimited inclusiveness, an invitation in every passage to enter the poem bringing my own *immediate* circumstances along with me. It seems beautiful to me that when I remember my first reading of almost any Ashbery piece, I remember my own situation at the time intermingled with the figures and gestures of the poem. And as the effect is beautiful, it is one I desire for my own poetry. The undeclared intention leaves open the possibilities of new hybrid intentions, and makes of saying an escape from what I merely meant to say. Ambition delays meaning in order to mean more largely, more generously, abetted by the necessary co-operation of the reader who must bring his or her own circumstances to bear in order to read at all. Reading "Illustration," I am entirely free to determine the implications of an "effigy of indifference," just as I am free to judge the distance or nearness of such a Beckettian finality as resonates in "because it is the end." In writing, Ashbery teaches me to desire not an increase in my individual portion of imaginative freedom, but an increase in the stock of freedom available to anyone.

> "... There is nothing to do
> For our liberation, except wait in the horror of it.
>
> And I am lost without you."
> ("They Dream Only of America")

Because freedom is intentionless, its accomplishment, "our liberation," requires nothing of us. Yet in a further variation of inversion technique, Ashbery establishes this nothing as neither nugatory nor still. It requires great effort, a redoubling of negative capability, to articulate phrases, lines, and stanzas without resort to the reassurances and little victories of expressed intent. That is why Ashbery poises the line "There is nothing to do" as a positive, proposing absolute indeterminacy as a task – the nothing that somehow *must* be done. Here, as everywhere in *The Tennis Court Oath*, Ashbery reminds me that the imagination is not an inward quality in search of expression, but rather, an event that occurs when perception contacts the world with the force of desire in the form of words or paint or sounds. Imagination defines itself in what it does, participating in liberty *as* liberty. Desire declares the unsatisfactoriness of the present moment (emotion "re-collected" is not emotion) and directs the mind towards its liberation from that state. And where can the mind go but to the world, and how can it travel but indeterminately, dissatisfaction being the sum of what has been determined? Just as "nothing" is a task, so waiting is an activity, a pioneering. The imagination happens, poems happen in the time pried open by waiting, time made porous to accidents and new juxtapositions by the deferral of particularity. There, words contrive new syntaxes and thus new meanings because none has been prescribed. There, the mind moves more ways than one. This multiplicity is the primary prerequisite of imagination, a "horror" owing to the utter defenselessness it prolongs. Where there is no horror, no uninterpreted, there is only the awful and unacceptable condition of certainty: that isolated, final, and feckless utterance "And I am lost without you." If I have no single destination, I cannot be lost, only en route. As long as I am waiting, anything may yet arrive. As America failed in the moment it became an ideality instead of a plurality of discrete then overlapping events (a city on a hill instead of an explorer's beautiful misinterpretation), voices and poems fail when they reconcile themselves to a solitary posture. Closure victimizes thought. *Something* victimizes the *nothing* in which and by which our liberation persists. Every final word expresses defeat. John Ashbery does not deny that a final word always gets said. The trick is to prolong the dream, the recital, the ice storm-all the unfinished originals. The trick is to write as far into the accidents as one can before collapsing into statement. Poetry stops where nothing cannot be said any longer or in only one way: "And I am lost without you."

> I prefer "you" in the plural, I want "you,"
> You must come to me, all golden and pale
> Like the dew and the air
> And then I start getting this feeling of exaltation.
> ("A Blessing in Disguise")

The actual implementation of delay and the exercise of desire in the widest time, the broadest space, depend upon a form of stubbornness. ("Virtue is only stubbornness," as Ashbery writes in "The Picture of Little J.A. in a Prospect of Flowers.") As here the voice insists upon the plurality of its desired object, I have learned to do my best to maintain the variousness of any subject, to be greedy on behalf of my figures, to want them visible and elusive, vivid and imprecise. We are used to thinking of clarity as a kind of focus. Yet in placing desire at the heart of his technique, Ashbery opts for the clarity of expansiveness, a kinetic rather than a pictorial apprehension of whatever the imagination finds or makes desirable. Such stubbornness refuses to privilege the spatial distinctions to which most poems aspire; it slides away from the epiphanic representation, from the brilliant immanence of things such as Lowell's aquarium in its Sahara of snow, preferring instead a presentational restlessness, a sequence not of images but of qualities. Thus, "You must come to me," not in a specific form, but "golden" and "pale." It is the goldenness and the paleness that matter; beside them the simile "like the dew and the air" seems as arbitrary and behind hand as all similes truly are in the context of desire. The presentational has neither time nor appetite for similes. Its feelings and objects rely upon whatever succeeds them or is summoned by them for their measure of clarity. (We all, John Ashbery included, owe much to Frank O'Hara for his courage in displacing traditional simile and metaphor with a distinctive, kinetic next-ness. I don't think he was kidding when, in "Personism: A Manifesto," he expressed the rationale of his technique by saying "If you're going to buy a pair of pants you want them to be tight enough so everyone will want to go to bed with you." The life of anything in a poem rests not with the thing itself but with what comes next because of it or with what is drawn to it by whatever qualities it exerts.) If I am, for example, writing about a woman looking at paintings in a gallery, I have learned from Ashbery not to picture her, but to follow her from canvas to canvas, taking pleasure and desiring even more pleasure because of her inexpressive momentum, the way she takes the qualities of one painting along with her, momentarily, into her confrontation with the next painting and so on. And as pleasure always feels itself to be (rightly or wrongly) a beginning rather than an ending, the first in a series of sensations rather than the last, this kinetic technique allows for satisfaction with no con-current diminishment of appetite, with no loss of momentum or potential for variation. Ashbery writes "And then I *start* getting this feeling of exaltation." Until the inevitable final word, the poem's last sensation, the virtue of stubbornness keeps the poem in step with and indistinguishable from everything available to it in time.

> Mixed days, the mindless years perceived
> With half-parted lips
> The way the breath of spring creeps up on you and floors you.
> ("The Double Dream of Spring")

The language of stubbornness catalogues more than it defines. This is the use of appetite, for motivation. We have all lived "mixed days" and we can all, usually to our regret, look back on "mindless years." Yet we cannot literally picture them, and my mixed days and mindless years cannot serve as paradigms for anyone else's. Ashbery insists that time is physical, is flavored and textured, that it is more than a site to be occupied or observed. Perception happens in the mouth, tasting and speaking simultaneously so as to elide the distortions of reflections and memory. Perception of this kind can never be offered up as figurative; poet and reader are simply carried along by it to make of it what they can in each other's company, but individually. What Ashbery recommends here, "with half-parted lips," is *not* automatic writing. His destination is the entire actual, not the secret cloister of the unconscious. I believe he recommends that the poet write *with* instead of *about* moments of being. (Think of the curtains that keep blowing in "The System.") Image and symbol translate perception into repeatedly accessible forms. "Mixed days" and "mindless years perceived / With half-parted lips" arrive purely as themselves, still in flux, not to be consulted but to be completed by every individual reading in countless unprepared ways. As Breton insisted, automatic writing is absolutely unalterable. The writing in "The Double Dream of Spring" changes with every reading because of the inherent incompleteness and stubborn provisionality of its figures. In automatic writing, the unconscious exerts total authority. In an Ashbery poem, authority is conjured in process, in the extent to which an intimate verisimilitude arises and is maintained between poet and reader as each continues through the poem, nurturing it with his own appetite, completing it with his own provisional conclusions. It invents a kind of faith: seeing with no evidence of having seen, knowing without any fixed points of reference. When I write with such a faith, I can make a phrase such as "the color of windows" or "the anatomies of the wind" and, without qualifying it further or locating it in any particularized context, poise it in my syntax as a finished statement rather than a phrase. It is what the speaker *is*, not merely what he sees. Windows have color, and the wind has body, but a person must be in their presence or imagine their presence to know them. Thus, to read my phrase is to join me somewhere, not to receive a message from me. And you will know the place in your own terms, having had no further terms from me.

The language of stubbornness speaks every way at once so as to leave the invitation of each phrase open. The recognizably poetic diction of "The way the breath of spring" slides without transition into the slightly vulgar, out-of-date colloquial of "creeps up on you and floors you." Too many poems have made an institution out of spring, a trope. Here the season is returned to time and arrives as it truly always does, as an overwhelming surprise. To try to say everything, one must be willing to use *all* the words in any truthful combination. In these opening lines of "The Double Dream of Spring" Ashbery invents my Realism.

> At once the weight of the other years and above all
> the weight of distinguishing among them slipped away.
> You found yourself not wanting to care.
>   ("The New Spirit")

In "Why I Am Not a Painter," Frank O'Hara writes "it is even in / prose, I am a real poet." And again, I don't think he was kidding, for surely it is the prose poem that has done the most to revivify the genres of poetry in our avant gardes. Rimbaud, Fargue and Jacob took the line away from the lyric and opened it to unmeasured tempi. This "other tradition" as Ashbery calls it in his book-length prose poem *Three Poems* reaches our own poetry through the innovations of Williams's *Kora in Hell* and in the collagings of his *Paterson*, thriving and diversifying now in the work of Edson, Simic, Tate, Berg and others. So it is not really surprising to me that I have, from among all of Ashbery's books, learned the most and continue to be the most influenced by *Three Poems*, never mind the fact that I have never written a prose poem. The literal feeling of reading *Three Poems* is a shocking education: the eyes move over page after page, sliding coolly over a surface of pronouns without antecedents, imagining nothing in particular, following no single train of thought; but when those eyes lift from the page, the room is changed, the world is changed. Ashbery's words suddenly adhere to the reader's surroundings. In this way, *Three Poems* is nothing *but* influence; the poem happens in the moment when the reader turns away from the poem. *Three Poems* models an insinuating fluent mundo of delay and stubbornness: the poem as more than object, more even than experience. It models a new means of experiencing, a new head.

The notion that a poem need not address itself to the clarification or elaboration of some property of mind, circumstance or heart, but can instead assume the status of otherness – subjectless and therefore equal to poet and reader alike – thrills and refreshes me. It has always seemed to me that to read is to choose to be an other: not necessarily an other or fictional character, but oneself reconfigured by new words and new combinations. In making a poem, a poet unburdens the language of its "distinguishing" utility, its syntactical atomizing, letting the words cluster as they do in each of us, vagrantly, uncaptioned, but with the integrity of selves. Too many poems deteriorate into puzzles, feeling themselves captured at some point by an emerging identity to which they must supply a local habitation and a name, a "solution." But the self, the *tourbillon* of phrases moving consciously and unconsciously headlong in time, is not restricted by identity in any such mechanical way. It can and does mix its metaphors shamelessly. Its antecedents are rarely certain. To paraphrase Ashbery's "Soonest Mended," a self is, and therefore a poem can be, an "emulsion," a suspension of undissolved, unreconciled particles in unstable relationship one to another. When I write a poem, I find myself "not wanting to care," urgently desiring the carelessness to say and believe what I need not explain or understand. And if I write to be someone else and not merely someone else's, the writing must be careless lest it be captured by the rhetoric of solution. Think of the beautiful passage from *Paterson* Book III: "Only one answer: write carelessly so that nothing that is not green will survive."

> It is the lumps and trials
> That tell us whether we shall be known
> And whether our fate can be exemplary, like a star.
>   ("The One Thing that Can Save America")

Where the technique is carelessness, the medium (that which provides the passing forms of the beautiful) is recklessness. In an Ashbery poem, time subjects the improvisations of language – selves, desires, attitudes, dreams – to "lumps and trials." The success of any improvisation, its material viability over time, depends on the results of these trials, upon what literally happens to it in the open field of collisions and reorientations that is the poem as a whole. Ashbery's art is thus materialistic in the most fundamental sense: what a poem is made of is what a poem means. Williams calls for such materialism in *Paterson*, "a poetry / of the movements of cost." Some figures go unresolved or disappear entirely, eroded into irrelevance or nothingness by the exigencies of their "fate"; others survive, not necessarily intact or unchastened, but competent to change and still illuminating, "exemplary, like a star" in that a star, even as it dies, offers light and direction and the indeterminate thrill of its unique, remote possibilities. Every poem eventually abandons its figures, either by ending or by taking up new figures *in medias res*. Value arises from duration or intensity, as it does with stars, and so value evidences itself as a function of materiality, a quality of cost. For example, "Syringa" sends an Orpheus entirely its own into "the nature of things to be seen only once, / As they happen along, bumping into other things." This Orpheus proves most adaptable, shifting and changing his songs to extol and then to exhaust many measures of art, nature, love, and time. And in the end, he is not torn apart; rather, he is simply used up, burned out like a star, and the poem continues to its finish without its Orpheus and yet with something of the beauty of his example, his fatal trajectory. Orpheus "is no longer / Material for a poem," and so the poem finds other material. The reckless economy of poetry teaches that "Stellification / Is for the few," that out of many figures, only a handful resonate with enough life in enough time to set us the kind of example, i.e. an exemplary self, in search of which we originally resort to the writing and reading of poems. In order to find these, the imagination tries and squanders a great deal, living carelessly off its only capital: the real and real time. The compact measures of bad poetry are niggardly; they refuse to waste words and try to pass off such parsimony as virtue. Ashbery has taught me that I *must* waste words, lots of them, trying them against and upon one another, allowing them and their syntaxes to fall apart sometimes in order to find not the true ones, but the ones that seem true at the time, the ones whose example I am willing to follow to their ultimately silent ends. The wasting and the falling apart are the circumstances, the medium of poetry. Goethe's Faust enters history at the moment he defines *logos* as action. To offer merely the frugal artifact despairs of beauty in advance.

> You can't say it that way any more.
> ("And *Ut Pictura Poesis* Is her Name")

Despair acquiesces to repetition and submits the imagination to unacceptable archetypes. The poetics of despair practice a museum-shop mimesis, producing reproductions of what is no longer reproductive. The vernal influence of John Ashbery does not traffic in despair, and in the piece closest to an *ars poetica* of any he has made, the freedoms of the stubbornly careless voice break the mimetic open at both ends, celebrating the liberty of subject in one direction and object in another. The imagination is no mirror, and the world is no image. In every passage of "And *Ut Pictura Poesis* Is her Name," words resonate and combine in more ways than any merely harmonious syntax could contain. As John Cage has suggested, in the new music every instrument is a percussion instrument. Thus "She approached me / About buying her desk. Suddenly the street was / Bananas and the clangor of Japanese instruments." In the logic of percussion, one sound follows another and that is all. The effect created depends entirely upon the intensity and materiality of a collision; the context is an event of impact, not a prescribed tonality. Mimesis assumes that understanding is the true end of imagination, that reality can be captured. Ashbery continually gives evidence to the reverse: imagination is the *literal end* of understanding ("so that understanding / May begin and in doing so be undone"), and in poetry, reality escapes capture, accompanied and abetted by the percussion of language and thought. The profligate waste of words in an open field of collisions ("an almost empty mind / Colliding with the lush, Rousseau-like foliage") increases the real by unframing it, increases the personae of syntax by unsubordinating them to copywork.

But it's all there in that very fist line: "You can't say it that way anymore." Whoever you are, whatever it was you wanted to say in whatever way you had wanted to say it, will no longer suffice. Between the intention and the act falls not a shadow, but the entire world, and it isn't just falling but moving around like crazy. Intentionality (mimesis & co.) is a hollow-man's self-mocking isolation. The reckless abandonment of intention's mimetic typography closes the gap between the poem and the world, between the desire to make and the desire to be remade. Ashbery replaces mimesis with amazement without recourse to Dadaist excess, but via a constant preparedness to be unprepared by the next word, the next phrase, the next situation, however homely or extravagant. The courage to write the next word even and especially when it contradicts all the words preceding it opens a poem to the beautiful by freeing it from the picturesque. "You can't say it that way anymore" resonates for me in the ways in which I imagine Rilke's "You must change your life" resonated for poets earlier in this century. Change is only terrible when it has been prescribed or when its outcome is foreknown. When reckless, when arbitrary, change liberates possibility from precedent, and that is the highest purpose of action that I know. I learn from Ashbery that the technique of poetry is an unstyling, the conquest of fidelity by desire.

What need for purists when the demotic is built to last,
to out outlast us, and no dialect hears us?
("Purists Will Object")

Poetry works on principles of dispossession, resisting pressures to convert desire into acquisitiveness. Ashbery's profoundest influence makes itself felt in the ways in which he discovers motives and momentums of desire in language itself, the inclination of words and phrases themselves to forsake what is merely available in favor of what might be made available by new expressions, the undetermined sponsors of new selves and new ways of perceiving. If, as Rimbaud avows, life is elsewhere, then desire is our only birth and new expression our only vitality. Ashbery is no *enfant terrible*; his restless originality feels to me more like tenderness than like the shock of the new, a tenderness inclined to the nurturing of time's timeliness and to an attentive love for the ephemeral which is, after all, everything. All purists are reductive, enslaved by their exclusive versions of a golden age. Theirs is the poetry of re-enactment, curiously imperious and irrelevant at one and the same time. But the demotic, the popular songs and showtunes whose ephemera Ashbery's voices remember to love, expresses the unchaste, entirely innocent activity of time whose compounding of more accidents, intentions and events than any one self or design could possibly comprehend is the supremest fiction, unimperious and not at all fictitious. The demotic is "built to last" because it is never finished, cannot even conceive of finishing. Acknowledging no distinction between being and making, its expressions assume the momentary to be larger than eternity, its reaches wider, its improvisations more compelling than the claustral gestures of any heaven. The momentary demotics "outlast us," and to keep pace with them, poets must dispossess themselves continuously of selves and symbols or else risk the aphasia of pure design.

I've said that influence is disturbance. Writing this sequence of little meditations, I've remembered that disturbance is excitement and that Ashbery excites me most with his insistence that the language is always somewhere ahead of me, that "no dialect hears" me because the endless improvisation of any dialect's existence has no time to reflect upon my reflective self. The word I am looking for, which is of course always the next word, is nowhere to be found. It is, instead, waiting to happen and then happening now.

The Moving Sidewalk

*The sleepwalking child opens his eyes
and realizes he is sleeping.*
　　　　　— Jean-Paul Sartre, *Saint Genet*

To write is to steal a word or, better, to steal into the word and then out again. Years later, I am answering a woman whose name I never learned. Once, at a convention of teachers, I gave a talk, and when I'd finished, she rose and denounced my university appointment as unjust and oppressive because it ought by valid, revisionary right to be held by someone other than a white male. I remember wanting to answer that she had mistaken me, that I was not a member of the *class* to which she had referred. But I said nothing or, perhaps, something frivolous, something worse than nothing. Nevertheless, in America, where skin has always been a kind of money, and color the confidence and translucence of value, class is an *ethnic* origin. I want to answer the woman, to say that mine is not the whiteness she imagined.

Man is the only creature who refuses to be what he is.
　　(Albert Camus, *The Rebel*)

My experience, a refraction of class, originated and continues in a border region between writing and the class-fantasies of language. Sometimes complementary, sometimes violently conflicted, these fantasies subjugate my sense of myself to local histories. At times simultaneous, at times mechanically sequential, the fantasies also isolate my life from the life of the times. I have traversed these *particular* delusions alone. No official categories explain my ghosts to me.

I was born white and male, baptized and raised as an Episcopalian. According to my schoolbooks, according to the media, I governed and thrived. Mine was the typology of the Founding Fathers whose symbols exercised great power in maximum liberty. But circumstances ruptured the words from the meanings, the promises. I lived in the South Bronx, then and now a disfigured expanse of abandoned fires and helpless cruelties. Environment obviated my power, my liberty, making phantoms of the words to which I was born. Whiteness confined and exposed me to the perils of minority. America might have been a white people's nation, but in the Bronx, whiteness signified a freakish shame: the skin that failed. Blacks and Hispanics lived there because of external oppressors and prejudice. *I* was there because my family somehow lacked or had dissipated the advantage of its color. My whiteness was a blank prey made even more superfluous by its gender.

And my privileged religion lay confined within a confinement, isolating me from the few other whites nearby. (For the most part, our parishioners came from far outside the community, bound to an isolated landmark by sentiment or habit.) Our white neighbors were Irish Catholics. Enrolled in marginalized parochial schools, their children were as carapaced by oppression as were the Blacks and Hispanics, as insulted by my established faith as others were by the perforated fiction of my skin. The refuge of church became a prank of words: children marching beneath the el and singing of the Saints "at sea, in shops, in lanes, or at tea." The language grew hilarious with anachronism, more an inverted minstrel show than a form of worship.

In the Bronx, fantasy deformed the background as well as the foreground language of daily life. The absurdity of me convulsed in a surround of absurdities. My street was Beach Avenue although it neither touched nor imagined any shore. To the east, Soundview had no view of Long Island Sound or of anything but a further range of tenements. In the west, absolutely treeless, Longwood dropped into the gorge of an expressway. The words on my birth certificate kept none of their promises. The words on the street signs kept none of their promises. Nothing possessed the presumptive nature of its name.

My life began as gibberish, a fantasy cordoned off by traffic. It abjected every word I knew or learned. And if somehow I became a writer, I should be obliged to understand this abjection by interrogating the class formulae of its means. Is writing the perpetuation of a received fantasy, an eloquent submission to class, or is it an exposure, a flaying? And if the fantasy is dispelled, can something larger than a self-made fantasy, a hermetic fiction of freedom, be spoken it its place?

To hope for reality is to hope for a classless word and, in Camus' sense, to rebel against identity.

> The true pleasure of a thief becomes a fictive pleasure of a fake owner. Reality is worn so thin that one can see the light through it.
> (Sartre, *Saint Genet*)

Rebellion entails the conscious and half-conscious refusal of many virtues. Early, I believed that my imagination could steal into the language and empowerment of a criminal class, a class which, refusing the sanctions of property, invents a world exterior to the one in which humans are assorted by legitimate property and human words eviscerated by deluded, dutiful aspiration. (Why *should* Beach Avenue dream of a shoreline?) I had the example of my father to inspire me. From boyhood, he'd been a thief and an expediter of thefts. Illiterate, inelegant, and untraveled, he nevertheless, because of his physical strength, his savvy and his rumored friendship with criminal big shots, acquired great prestige in my eyes. He knew the owners and the backrooms of stores, and when we visited we never left without our little gifts. His exemption from ordinary labor seemed like a kind of grace to me, his crimes alchemical escapes from the machinery of getting, spending, and being spent. He wielded the power of the outside as an outsider.

Predictably then, one ambition of my poems was to write the outside, to move from the embrace of theft, the brute unsanctioning of legitimacy, into an outsider's empowerment. I imagined a poem of thuggery, of shock and escape in the aftershock. I took the Beats for models and, by vigorously misreading *A Season in Hell*, used Rimbaud as a catalyst in the redaction of spite into freedom. Crime transforms the *enfant terrible* into the *enfant libre*, or so I and all who have indulged the fantasy of a criminal class once believed. But a painful claustrophobia undoes the fantasy, exposing its power as fakery. As I matured, I learned that my father was literally a nobody outside the narrow circuit of his thefts and that he was as confined by that circuit as by a cell. He sat in our apartment amidst the rubbish of his gifts. Because nothing had been paid for, nothing could be repaired, and so our family depended totally upon opportunity and upon accidents of intimidated largesse. We had things free, but we had few choices. The neighborhood thief steals neighborhood property, and in the Bronx, property was meager and unreliable.

Likewise, it was not long until I felt the claustrophobia of poetic thuggery. Shock, as a method, is abjected to the comfortable superiority of its audience; the Beats were the zoo creatures of American prosperity. Crime is a backward alchemy that reduces human will to parasitism, and Rimbaud escapes my early, criminal misreading by achieving a will to love greater than any insulted caprice. The thief's exemption signifies ultimate exclusion. My fantasy of a transcendent criminal class reacted but did not rebel against the gibberish of my birth.

> Morality, when it is formal, devours.
> (Camus, *The Rebel*)

Time mocks the pretense of temporal prepositions. Whether class-paradigms of escape overlapped, displaced, or partnered one another in The Bronx seems unimportant as compared to the strong impulse that surrendered me to them. During the same years in which I tested a thief's transcendence, I sought a different kind of escape: a refuge in the sheltering fantasy of the *insider*. A criminal steals into power by violating the propriety of words and actions, exteriorizing them in the name of chaos. The presumptive insider steals into security by imitating the formal proprieties of repression, interiorizing them in the name of order. The insider is a shadow cast by his own abjection, and a collective of these, a shadow-class, is a gang.

Insubstantial but violent, a gang member imitates the forms of the society that denies his existence. In the absence of community, he is initiated and he initiates. In the absence of a cause, he makes war. In the absence of justice, he condemns and is condemned. I thought that in a gang I would be empowered by protection. Acceding to its rituals, its rules and gratuitous enmities, I would acquire the status of priest, policeman, and warrior. "Better to reign in Hell than serve in Heaven." Milton's demons were a gang, and as with all gangs, they were a parody of what had expelled them. A gang is a manifestation of shame and inadequacy. In The Bronx, our imitations of order postponed an understanding: traditional order itself had engineered the terrors that drove us into gangs. A gang completes the erasure of identity begun by misfortune, and so it is a violence practiced on itself. Entering a gang, a nobody becomes a nothing with a bold new name.

One day, a member of our gang was ambushed by rivals and badly beaten. He told us afterwards that the attackers had been led by Ace, someone we all knew by sight and reputation. We fulminated and planned, and in a few days three of us managed to capture Ace when he was alone. We took him behind a broken wall and nearly killed him. I remember beating his face with my belt buckle until his face was gone. We took his jacket and left him. In a ceremony that night, we tore it into pieces, and the patch that bore his name, "Ace," was stitched onto *my* jacket. On behalf of a fiction, one shadow had stolen another shadow's fictive name. In the whole business, the only realities were wounds, humiliations, and the disfigurement of a boy whose actual name I never learned. And I have yet to lean the extent to which I was myself disfigured behind the broken wall.

The shadow impulse, the shamed violence of imitation, endured in me. It survived good fortune that took me out of The Bronx, and it survived my education into the securities of adult life. I know that it disfigured many years of reading, disguising envy as admiration. For example, when I first read the poems of Auden and Bogan, I understood their eloquence to be the gestures of a perfect complacency, their forms to be the ceremonies of unafflicted invention. I envied their facility too much to recognize (or to emulate) the courage of their minds or the deep colors of their humility. Disfigured reading makes for disfigured writing, and I know that many of the poems in my first book, *From the Abandoned Cities*, adopted traditional forms out of an impulse to feign a distance I did not feel and a manner I merely envied. I stole into formalism as I had stolen Ace's jacket; my measured stanzas were as abject as the ritual of tearing the jacket and sewing its name onto my own. Form gave me the illusion of control and escape. It made me feel like an insider, an initiate of mysteries, sheltered from chaos. But my poems were false interiors. They arranged but did not explain the violence of their origins or the dysfunction of their words. They recounted much, but they accounted for nothing. The shadow-class of the gangs remained their source. Contrived, not made, their music was a self-devouring silence.

Love is the entranced morality that served this exile as a native land.

(Camus, *The Rebel*)

It has been difficult for me to speak of origins because I'm eager to believe that my real origins are still ahead. In resisting difficulty, I have been aided by a dialogue between two great books, *Saint Genet* and *The Rebel*, each of which confronts the oppressiveness and the inadequacy of class as a reading of human circumstance. Class oppresses because it is a categorical starvation of our actual lives and actual words. And class is an inadequate category because its fantasies can hardly begin to explain the admixtures of anguish and rapture in a human life. Sartre offers the model of Genet, "comedian and martyr," in answer to class. Theft and the impersonation of identity annihilate its authority, its interpretive stature, and in the ensuing void we may freely re-invent ourselves, unburdened of class. Camus offers the model of the Rebel, the individual who resists by means of constantly examined, constantly refreshed solidarity with all people: an intimation indivisible by class. In the end, I prefer Camus. His is a struggle free of resentment, and in my life too much and too many days have already been ruined by resentful thefts and flights, by the vengeful cowardice composed and imposed by class. There is a better entrancement than The Bronx, a better origin of myself and what I write, one that yet does not depend upon the circumstance of my birth.

I can find this entrancement in a particular memory. My first trip in an airplane brought me to New York from Atlanta. My father worried about the flight, and though he had never been to an airport, he wanted to meet me to see me safely landed. I came out of the jetway and could not find him. After a fretful search, I spotted him on the concourse below me, bewildered on a moving sidewalk, his dark face wetted with tears. Because the airport was well beyond the circuit of his crimes, because he could not read the monitors to find my gate, because the fantasy of his power made it impossible to ask for help, he was helplessly lost. Seeing him that way, I felt a strange liberty whose meanings I've tried to unpuzzle ever since. My father, largest emblem of all my origins, the nearest human figure of my class, could not find me. What he symbolized was insufficient to define me, and what does not define me cannot oppress me. Seeing him helpless, I did not feel a rage at injustice. I did not feel pity of the need to invent a fantasy to dignify his tears. I felt free, and free, I could love my father.

Writing is the central activity of my life. Because my father, my original, cannot read, there is no hope and no danger of my ever winning his approval. From this I extrapolate that my poems need never struggle in the backward of my beginnings. My life in The Bronx is as helpless as my father on the moving sidewalk, and I am at liberty to think of poetry not as theft nor as a shadow power, but as an act of love: an unrehearsed, unclarifying, unstructuring summons to the summons of the present moment. Class is an understanding best refused, an explanation best forgotten. In the sudden gratuitousness of forgetting and living without its pathos and schema, I can read and write freely. My models now are the beautiful carelessness of William Carlos Williams and the surface lights of Gertrude Stein. If my father finds me, it is because I call.

Coda

Dear Friend

I must tell you I can never think of Poetry as anything but a loving power, a god who sometimes visits me and visits you along its bright unfolding way. It seems quite fine to me that Jack Spicer called these visits "dictations," and equally fine that William Blake should choose words like "Everlasting Gospel." A poem is the efflorescence of a power, evidence of something whose purpose is, I truly believe, our happiness and even our delight.

And so invited to offer advice to poets younger then myself, I choose a text whose pretext is just such happiness: powerful, sudden, and shared. I'm saying I carry a poem in my pocket. It's not a mantra or a model. It's good news and evidence. These days, it's a later poem of William Carlos Williams' – "Iris."

> a burst of iris so that
> come down for
> breakfast
>
> we searched through the
> rooms for
> that
>
> sweetest odor...
>
> . . . .
>
> ...then a blue as
> of the sea
> struck
>
> startling us from among
> those trumpeting
> petals

All the reminders and advice I could hope to share are here. (And, of course, elsewhere – always a good idea to change the poem in your pocket to remember poetry never changes.) And so, again to begin:

A poet, whatever else he or she may be, is not a creative writer. As Emily Dickinson opined, "Unto the Whole – how add?" The world creates itself, and poetry is pleased to show its new creation to our words. Williams'"burst of iris" is the author of the poem. What Williams writes is the record of its authority and of his coming to his senses, all of which lead to an iris.

And so, clearly, there's no need for imagination. It would be a downright hindrance. The poem is entirely of its real place and moment. Nothing is missing which imagination might supply. Write where you are. Our art is simply one form of attention, a going out to meet the world that comes so freely, so effortlessly to us and to our senses. It would be an effort not to smell the "sweetest odor," an effort not to seek its "startling" source. Imagination is just such an effort, and who needs it as long as there are flowers?

Always welcome distraction. Remember Baucis and Philemon. They were eternally rewarded. William's poem is one delighted upshot of distraction, something much better than the breakfast for which he'd come downstairs. You cannot come to your senses by closing your ears and eyes. Poets don't need Retreats; they advance. Poetry is a wild god, and our piety consists of an always grateful bewilderment. (I love the 17th century form of "bewildered," i.e. "bewildernessed!") To be amazed, one must enter, willingly if unintentionally, a maze. Think of the first line of John Ashbery's "Some Trees:" "These are amazing." And God knows what prolixities "Kubla Khan" might have sunk beneath without the blessed haphazard of a person from Porlock. After all, it was the same Coleridge who found himself redeemed by distraction in his great "Dejection: An Ode." A raving wind blew him out of his mind and into the next valley, where he was loved. Leave the window open. Answer the door. Catching the fragrance of a flower, go and find it.

I come to a plain distinction, and there, I find, is everything I know about being a poet. There is mind, and there is mindfulness. Throw away your mind; it is a ragbag of wishes and words. Mind can only recognize the wearing and worn-out measures of itself. If you find yourself in a cave, you needn't unpuzzle the shadows on the wall. Turn yourself round and walk into the sunshine making them. I forget what wonderful American preacher it was who once said "If you find you're rubbing the cat the wrong way, turn the cat around." Whoever he was, he knew a very great deal about Poetry. He was mindful. Mindfulness has eyes that can be surprised by joy. It can find an iris.

Donald Revell is Professor of English and Director of Creative Writing Programs at the University of Utah. Twice winner of the PEN Center USA Award for Poetry, he has also won the Academy of American Poets' Lenore Marshall Prize and is a former fellow of the Ingram Merrill and Guggenheim Foundations. Additionally, he has twice been granted fellowships in poetry from the National Endowment for the Arts. Former editor-in-chief of *Denver Quarterly*, he now serves as poetry editor of *Colorado Review*. Revell lives in the desert south of Las Vegas with his wife, poet Claudia Keelan, and their children Benjamin Brecht and Lucie Ming.

green press

INITIATIVE

Omnidawn Publishing is committed to preserving ancient forests and natural resources. We elected to print *Invisible Green* on 50% post consumer recycled paper, processed chlorine free. As a result, for this printing, we have saved:

5 trees (40' tall and 6-8" diameter)
2,046 gallons of water
823 kilowatt hours of electricity
226 pounds of solid waste
443 pounds of greenhouse gases

Omnidawn Publishing made this paper choice because our printer, Thomson-Shore, Inc., is a member of Green Press Initiative, a nonprofit program dedicated to supporting authors, publishers, and suppliers in their efforts to reduce their use of fiber obtained from endangered forests.

For more information, visit www.greenpressinitiative.org

Library of Congress Cataloging-in-Publication Data

Revell, Donald, 1954-
    Invisible green : selected prose of Donald Revell.
        p. cm.
    ISBN-13: 978-1-890650-22-3 (acid-free paper)
    ISBN-10: 1-890650-22-6 (acid-free paper)
    I. Title.
    PS3568.E793I585 2005
    814'.54--dc22

                                        2005015173